OVEREDUCATION IN THE U.S. LABOR MARKET

Russell W. Rumberger

foreword by
Henry M. Levin

PRAEGER

PRAEGER SPECIAL STUDIES • PRAEGER SCIENTIFIC

Library of Congress Cataloging in Publication Data

Rumberger, Russell W
    Overeducation in the U.S. labor market.

    Bibliography: p.
    Includes index.
    1. College graduates--Employment--United States.
2. Education, Higher--Economic aspects--United States.
3. Labor supply--United States. 4. Job satisfaction--
United States. I. Title.
HD6278.U5R85   331.11'423   80-24648
ISBN 0-03-057964-3

Published in 1981 by Praeger Publishers
CBS Educational and Professional Publishing
A Division of CBS, Inc.
521 Fifth Avenue, New York, New York 10175 U.S.A.

© 1981 by Praeger Publishers

123456789   145   987654321

Printed in the United States of America

To my parents,

Allen and Ellen Rumberger

FOREWORD

Henry M. Levin

In 1960 most college graduates had their choice of high-level
positions in both industry and government. Today many have difficulties finding full-time employment, and even more find themselves
relegated to jobs that were formerly filled by high school graduates.
This rather abrupt shift in the fortunes of the young has led to concern
about the possibility of overeducation. Historically, education was
viewed as an experience that one could never have enough of. It was
considered desirable for all: the more education one obtained, the
better. In part this view was attributable to the enduring romantic
vision of education held by people in the United States—that of creating
the good life. Education was considered the basis of democracy,
equality, prosperity, cultural progress, and technological advance.
Further, a rapidly growing economy—particularly in the post-World
War II period—created demands for an ever larger cadre of highly
skilled persons to fill technical, professional, and managerial occupational roles. Under such conditions, how could one conceive of a
phenomenon called overeducation?

But today the connection between a college education and the job
market, as well as other claims for an educated population, is increasingly questioned. In fact, some evidence shows that the economic, social, and political systems are simply unable to fill the high
expectations for status, income, and job satisfaction of so many college graduates. This dramatic historical change sets the stage for
the inquiry by Russell Rumberger. In this work he first raises the
question of what is meant by overeducation and suggests a number of
definitions. He then proceeds to demonstrate that different views of
the relation between education and the labor market create different
definitions and operational measures of overeducation.

After setting the conceptual framework, he proceeds to study the
relation between the skills required of jobs in the United States and the
skills reflected in the education of the U.S. labor force. Particularly
instructive is the study of changes in the skill requirements of jobs
between 1960 and 1976 as well as changes in the skill composition of
the increasingly educated labor force over that period. In making
these comparisons between the skills required of jobs and those possessed by job holders, several surprises emerge. Foremost is the
finding that jobs requiring the very highest level of skills are apparently diminishing, while the number of persons possessing such credentials is increasing dramatically. Further, given the disparity between the demands of employers for skills and the much larger sup-

ply of skilled persons as reflected in educational attainments, considerable overeducation does exist in the U.S. economy.

Rumberger concludes this study by exploring the consequences of overeducation on job satisfaction, productivity, and other measures of worker attitudes and behavior. He observes that overeducation may have a disruptive effect on production and may be a significant force for change in the U.S. workplace. The final chapter of the book explores the consequences of these findings for private and public policy.

In this book Rumberger presents a systematic analysis and evaluation of one of the major educational issues of our times. The presentation is straightforward, the analysis cogent and penetrating.

Henry M. Levin
Director, Institute for Research on
  Educational Finance and Governance
Professor, School of Education
Stanford University

ACKNOWLEDGMENTS

Support for this project was provided by the Employment and Training Administration, U.S. Department of Labor, under Research and Development Grant No. 91-06-77-23. Since grantees conducting research and development projects under government sponsorship are encouraged to express their own judgment freely, this report does not necessarily represent the official opinion or policy of the Department of Labor. The grantee is solely responsible for the contents of this report.

The Lucas data and the 1960 census data were generously supplied by the Center for Economic Studies. Computer-coded data for the third and fourth editions of the <u>Dictionary of Occupational Titles</u> and the cross-reference for the two editions were supplied by the U.S. Employment Service, Division of Occupational Analysis.

A number of people provided assistance and support for this project. The staff at the Stanford Center for Information Processing was extremely helpful in solving computer problems. I especially want to thank Larry Rosen. I benefited from discussions with Bill Behn and Joyce Crain at the Center for Economic Studies. Dortha Gilbert, Sherry McNamara, Ellen Mumma, and Julie Zavakos of the Center for Human Resource Research assisted with the preparation of the final manuscript. Finally, Laura Best provided technical, emotional, and philosophical support for me through the duration of this project.

Scholastic guidance was provided by a number of persons at Stanford. I would like to thank Martin Carnoy and Lewis Mayhew for serving on my reading committee. Andy Kolstad supplied me with useful information in the early stages of this project. Other faculty and students in the School of Education also provided their insights into the area of study pursued in this project.

Most of all, I would like to thank my adviser and friend, Henry Levin. Without his presence at Stanford I would probably not have continued my studies or developed an interest in the economics of education. He repeatedly provided guidance and direction throughout my years at Stanford, teaching me how to analyze problems, express ideas, and communicate my thoughts through writing. I would especially like to thank him for spending countless hours with me on this project.

CONTENTS

LIST OF TABLES

LIST OF FIGURES

PART I
INTRODUCTION

1

EXPLORING THE MEANING
OF OVEREDUCATION

For over three centuries, college graduates in the United
States have had a preferred place in the job market—more
interesting and prestigious jobs, higher incomes, less unemployment than the general population.

> Carnegie Commission on
> Higher Education, 1973

More Americans Take Jobs for Which They are Overqualified

> Wall Street Journal, January 16, 1976

How Valuable Is A College Degree?

> Columbus Dispatch, June 2, 1980

Until recently, it seems that few people ever questioned the
value of postsecondary education. Economists told us that educational
investment was partially responsible for the vast growth in the U.S.
economy; parents told us that it was the way to get ahead in life; government officials told us that it was good for our country; and school
officials told us that it would make better individuals. Scholars and
academics supported these notions by demonstrating that participation
in postsecondary schooling was a worthwhile endeavor, especially
since it assured success in the labor market in the form of high wages
and employment in high-status occupations (Becker 1975; Mincer 1974;
Blau and Duncan 1967).

The vast growth in the postsecondary educational system reflects this popular faith. Since World War II the system of postsecondary education has expanded at an unprecedented rate. Total expenditures increased from just over $4 billion in 1946 to over $121

billion in 1976, while the number of bachelor's degrees that were awarded increased eightfold during the same period (Grant and Lind 1979, pp. 27, 123). This vast growth resulted in a spectacular rise in the educational attainment of the population. For example, the number of young persons, 25 to 29 years of age, with a college degree increased threefold between 1950 and 1978 (Grant and Lind 1979, p. 16).

At the same time, the economy prospered. The size of the gross national product (in constant dollars) more than doubled between 1947 and 1977 (U.S., Department of Labor 1979, p. 385). This economic growth ensured appropriate jobs for college graduates who entered the labor market in the postwar period. The resulting growth in employment also favored those occupational categories that traditionally utilized college graduates. White-collar employment grew faster than blue-collar employment and became the predominant occupational sector.[1]

As evidenced, growth occurred in both the economic and educational sectors in the postwar period. From most accounts there were few problems in absorbing the influx of college graduates into the labor market.

Recent events, however, seem to contrast with this experience. Newspapers and magazines document accounts where college graduates are finding jobs of lower status and lower income than graduates of previous periods.[2] Scholars have presented empirical evidence suggesting that recent college graduates have not faired well in the labor market of the 1970s (Freeman 1975, 1976, 1977; Gordon 1974; Rumberger 1980). Both parents and students have begun to question whether a college education automatically guarantees the recipient a preferred place in the occupational hierarchy (Bird 1975). Faith in the value of postsecondary schooling has diminished.

The recent phenomenon of the plight of college graduates has been termed by some writers as overeducation. The term implies that the educational system is producing more college graduates than are socially useful. It suggests that the economic returns to an investment in schooling may be falling from their historically high levels. Exactly what is meant by "overeducation?" How can it be measured? Does a condition of "overeducation" exist in our society? Finally, if in fact "overeducation" does exist, what are the implications for individuals, for society, and for government policy?

This study will address these questions in an attempt to understand the phenomenon of "overeducation." The study has two major objectives. First, it will undertake a general discussion of the phenomenon of "overeducation."[3] In part because of the recent nature of this issue little discussion exists on the topic. It becomes clear from the existing literature that the term overeducation is associated with a variety of meanings and concerns. For example, some writers address the phenomenon simply from an economic perspective, analyzing changes in relative salaries among persons at different levels of educational attainment; others are concerned with society's investment in the educational enterprise and whether educated workers are underutilized in the economy; still others are concerned with the apparent decline of good jobs that are currently available to educated persons in comparison with the past. Regardless of how one defines overeducation, its existence could produce adverse effects in the workplace and have important implications for private and public policy. The complexity of these issues warrants a general discussion of overeducation.

The second objective of this study is to develop and apply one economic criterion of overeducation in order to measure the extent to which overeducation exists in the contemporary labor market. The empirical objective of this study is necessarily narrow. It will not concern itself with the value of education generally; this is a much broader question hampered by the methodological problem of measuring and quantifying the vast array of social and private benefits associated with educational outcomes. Rather, the analysis will concentrate on the function of education within the economic sphere of society. It is within this sphere that education is said to play an important role as a means of promoting social mobility and equality, as a means of allocating individuals to the most desirable and highest status jobs in society, and as an important factor in promoting economic growth.

The study is divided into three parts. Part I will consist of a general discussion of the topic of overeducation. The remainder of Chapter 1 will undertake a more general discussion of overeducation and then will explore some possible definitions of the phenomenon. Chapter 2 will discuss how the phenomenon of overeducation can be explained by alternative perspectives of the labor market.

Part II will constitute the empirical section of the study. Chapter 3 will outline the methodology. The empirical results, which measure the extent of overeducation in the contemporary labor market, will be presented in Chapter 4.

Part III will constitute the concluding section. Chapter 5 will explore the implications of overeducation for the workplace. Finally, Chapter 6 will discuss implications of overeducation for public and private policy as well as draw some general conclusions.

THE OUTCOMES OF OVEREDUCATION

Overeducation suggests that too much education is produced. To investigate such an allegation it is necessary to focus on the outcomes of education. It is well known that the educational enterprise produces many outcomes, although some are more prominent than others. These outcomes are often referred to as educational benefits. One benefit that results from investment in education is higher earnings. It is well documented that individuals with higher educational attainments earn on the average more than similar individuals with less schooling (Becker 1975; Mincer 1974). It is also known that individuals with more schooling are more likely to be employed in the higher-status professional and managerial occupations than persons with less schooling (Gordon 1974). Other benefits are less obvious and less documented. For example, proponents of increased public support for education argue that there is an array of benefits, including greater political participation and less crime (Withey et al. 1971; Bowen et al. 1977).

Educational benefits accrue to society as a whole as well as to the individuals who participate in the educational endeavor. The higher earnings of more-educated workers are obviously beneficial to those individuals, but they also contribute to the overall economy and the revenues of the government (Denison 1971; Bowman 1964). Some educational benefits accrue principally to the individual, such as the prestige of the job that the individual holds after finishing school. Other benefits accrue principally to society as a whole. Increased political participation and reduced crime not only benefit individuals but society in general.

Education produces many outcomes benefiting both society and individual participants. Overeducation suggests that too much education is being produced relative to what is necessary or efficient given its costs and benefits. For example, individuals often participate in the educational endeavor as an investment in their future well-being. There are costs incurred from such activity—direct costs, such as tuition charges, and indirect costs, such as incomes forgone while attending school. But there are also benefits expected from such participation, such as access to high paying jobs. Economists employ the technique of rate-of-return analysis to account for costs and benefits in order to measure the profitability of investment in education (Blaug 1970; Cohn 1975). Overeducation in these terms might exist if the rate-of-return to schooling for certain individuals fell below some predetermined level. That predetermined level must be suggested by those claiming the existence of overeducation.

More simply, overeducation could exist if the actual salary received upon completion of a given level of schooling fell below the expected level. For example, in a recent survey of college graduates, about two-thirds of those employed in areas outside of their field of study were earning less than they had expected; almost one-third of those employed in areas related to their field of study were earning less than they had expected (U.S., Bureau of Labor Statistics 1974a, p. A-12). One can think of overeducation in other ways. People may be overeducated if they are employed in occupations that fail to make use of all of the skills that they acquired in school.

From a social perspective, overeducation could exist in several ways. Some supporters of higher education argue that because social investment in education is in part justified owing to the social benefits it yields (for example, better political participation and reduced crime), there can never be too much education. Yet, these benefits involve costs to society. Overeducation can be considered in terms of a relative comparison of costs and benefits using rates-of-return, as in the individual case. In this instance the standard of comparison could be other social investments. If the social rate of return fell below the level of other social investments, one could argue that overeducation exists.

There is another way to view overeducation from a social perspective. If educated workers are underutilized in the workplace, and if those workers demonstrate poor work performance and high incidences of industrial conflict (for example, strike activity and industrial sabotage), then overeducation may have a negative social benefit.

To summarize, the phenomenon of overeducation can be viewed from either an individual or social perspective. This study will try to consider both. Overeducation may affect only certain individuals. At the same time, overeducated workers demonstrating adverse workplace behavior constitute a social problem as well.

The existence of overeducation does not call into question the benefits of the educational system generally, but rather, the benefits of education within the labor market. Consequently, this study will only address those aspects of educational benefits realized within the labor market. Such a restriction can be justified on several counts. First, it is within this sphere that overeducation has come to be recognized. The recent concern over the plight of college graduates, for example, has focused on labor market phenomena—the availability of jobs and the level of salaries. Second, public support of education is often justified by its economic contribution realized through the labor market activities of educated workers. Finally, individuals undertake investment in education in part for the benefits they expect will accrue to them within the labor market. This restriction does not discount the other benefits that result from education. Because of the importance of education in the labor market, the remainder of this study will be limited to the phenomenon of overeducation within this context.

SOME DEFINITIONS OF OVEREDUCATION

The preceding discussion suggested several ways that overeducation may exist within the labor market. In this section several alternative definitions of overeducation are discussed, including the conceptual advantages and disadvantages of each. In addition, evidence of overeducation based on each of the definitions is reviewed.

The forthcoming list of definitions is not exhaustive. It merely attempts to capture some common conceptions of what has been referred to as overeducation. It also does not preclude the possibility that this condition could exist according to several definitions simultaneously.

Declining Pecuniary Returns

The first definition deals with the higher earnings associated with more educated workers.

Definition 1: Overeducation exists when the pecuniary return to a particular level of schooling falls below its historically high level or declines relative to all other investments.

This definition can be used to evaluate overeducation from either a social or individual perspective. Based on this definition, individuals are considered overeducated if the return to their investment in a particular level of schooling either falls below the returns realized by similarly educated individuals in previous years or falls below the returns from other individual investments (for example, savings accounts). This definition can similarly be applied at a societal level for evaluating social investments in schooling. Social investment in education, based on the higher earnings and, consequently, the higher taxes of more educated individuals, can decline relative to other social investments or social returns enjoyed in the past.

This definition is based on an easily identified and widely accepted benefit of schooling—pecuniary remuneration. It has several conceptual shortcomings, however. Most important, pecuniary returns such as earnings are subject to forces of relative supply and demand that cause them to vary over time (Eckaus 1964). Rates-of-return fluctuate as well. With the utilization of education based on potentially varying remuneration, this definition may present an unstable and inaccurate picture of the value of education in the labor market.

Pecuniary returns also constitute only one criterion with which society can evaluate the profitability of social investments; that is, it is only one measure of usefulness or social value. In orthodox views of the labor market, pecuniary remuneration is related to individual contribution to the labor process. But as the discussion in the next chapter illustrates, it may not be a very accurate indication of individual productivity. There are also other social benefits from public investment in schooling that are not captured in pecuniary returns. So as a social criterion for measuring overeducation, this definition may be both imprecise and unstable. Similarly, as an individual criterion, it fails to capture the array of private benefits that result from individual investment in schooling (Duncan 1976; Lucas 1977).

Finally, a definition of overeducation based on pecuniary returns requires that some universal standard be applied to all individuals. There is no a priori reason why this should be the case. All individuals receiving similar pecuniary returns who are classified by this measure as being overeducated may not feel overeducated by their own personal evaluation. A universal standard of evaluation such as average returns in different periods of time does not account for individual variation or evaluation.

A definition of overeducation based on pecuniary returns presents methodological difficulties as well. First, it is often difficult to measure all pecuniary returns to schooling. Earnings may represent the principal component of pecuniary returns but there are other elements, such as pension, vacation, and medical benefits (Duncan 1976). Although accounting accurately for these other pecuniary benefits is more difficult, simply using earnings may understate the total benefits of schooling. Another difficulty arises in accounting for the actual returns. It is well known that the higher earnings of more-educated workers are not due solely to differences in the amount of schooling. For example, some of those differences may be due to differences in innate ability between more-educated and less-educated workers (Taubman and Wales 1975; Griliches 1977). To measure the true benefits of schooling requires an accounting of these factors.

In spite of its shortcomings, this measure has served as the basis of several studies that suggest overeducation exists in the labor market. Gordon (1974) notes that the ratio of incomes of college graduates to high school graduates increased steadily during the 1960s, a trend that was consistent for both males and females. In contrast, Freeman (1976) shows that the condition of college graduates worsened after 1969 as evidenced by a decline in the ratio of the average annual income of college graduates to the average annual income of high school graduates. Freeman (1975) also argues that this decrease in relative earnings resulted in a fall in the rate-of-return to investment in post-secondary education.

These studies are subject to the inherent weaknesses of this measure of overeducation. For example, even if the relative earn-

ings of college graduates declined in this period, this does not necessarily imply similar changes in other pecuniary or nonpecuniary benefits. More important, it is unclear whether there has been a significant deterioration of relative earnings for recent college graduates
(Grasso 1977; Rumberger 1980; Welch 1979). Evidence suggests that
a number of factors including a general economic decline influenced
both the supply and demand for educated workers in this period resulting in a relative economic decline for all young workers (Grasso 1977;
Smith and Welch 1978; Freeman 1979; Welch 1979). Furthermore, as
the next chapter points out, it is important to account for changes in
both relative and absolute salaries. Absolute salaries can decline
while relative salaries remain steady, causing social and private rates-
of-return to diverge.

In summary, a definition of overeducation based on earnings
presents a number of conceptual and methodological problems. It is
also unclear whether overeducation exists in the contemporary labor
market as defined by a fall in the pecuniary returns to schooling.

Unrealized Expectations

Another definition of overeducation is based on the degree to
which individuals realize their career expectations by participating
in the educational system. It applies primarily to those who volun-
tarily participate beyond the mandatory 12 years. Most students participating in postsecondary education do so with some expectation as
to what it may bring them in the future. Although education in economists' terms may have a consumption component, there is also an
investment component; individuals invest their time and money because
they expect to get something out of it. While such expectations may
not be limited to the labor market exclusively, at least some of them
undoubtedly are (Trent 1970). These expectations can serve as a
basis for defining overeducation.

Definition 2: Overeducation exists when an individual's expectations concerning the labor market benefits from an investment in
schooling are not realized.

Expectations may vary among individuals, reflecting individual variations in taste, aspirations, and circumstances. They may be related
to earnings, the status of jobs, or even particular jobs that an individual may expect after investing in a particular amount or kind of
schooling.

Again this concept may be used for evaluation from an individual
or a social perspective. It lends itself most appropriately as an in-

dividual measure because the evaluation of whether expectations are realized or not is an individual one. It functions as a social measure of overeducation through an aggregation of all those individuals who, through self-evaluation, qualify as overeducated. The most obvious advantage of this definition results from the individual evaluation of overeducation. Unlike the first definition, which requires some universal norm or standard, this one uses an individual standard. This feature makes it intuitively appealing since there is no reason one should expect two individuals with similar educational backgrounds in similar objective situations to feel the same about their positions in the labor market. It is more likely that their expectations are quite different and, hence, their reactions to similar objective situations are different as well. This definition also encompasses a larger spectrum of educational benefits, depending on how each individual evaluates them. For some, expectations may focus on pecuniary benefits; for others, they may be related to the type of job or the perceived status of the job.

Although a definition of overeducation based on individual expectations is intuitively appealing, it also presents problems. First, expectations are unstable; they may be revised as individual circumstances or personal traits (personality, interests, and so on) change. For example, individuals who enter college and aspire to be teachers may reevaluate their aspirations as the labor market for teachers changes. This definition may also be quite unsatisfactory as a social measure of overeducation. Pecuniary returns may not constitute a worthwhile measure of social value, but does the realization of expectations comprise a more worthwhile measure? It is unclear that it does. If workers expect promotions or other rewards by fulfilling what they believe are the necessary requirements (educational credentials), then failing to achieve those rewards may dash their expectations. Since unrealized expectations may create frustrated and dissatisfied workers, it may promote adverse behavior in the workplace (this topic is explored in Chapter 5). Thus, the relation of attainments to expectations for each level of education may serve as a useful barometer of overeducation.

Methodologically, it is obvious that this definition presents problems of measurement. The most straightforward way to measure overeducation by this definition is to ask everyone to evaluate themselves. But that may not be the most valid measure of unrealized expectations. Since expectations change over time, when is the time to measure unrealized expectations? Perhaps several measures would have to be employed over a period of time in order to account for changes in expectations.

The realization of expectations has not been used in any studies of overeducation thus far. Expectations, aspirations, and attitudes about jobs have been widely studied, however. This research suggests how a condition of overeducation could exist. For example, some studies focus on the expectations and attitudes of young people regarding work. After studying a series of surveys of youth between 1967 and 1973, Yankelovich (1974, p. 37) describes contemporary youth in the following manner:

> Today's generation of young people is less fearful of economic insecurity than generations in the past. They want interesting and challenging work, but they assume that their employers cannot—or will not—provide it. By their own say-so, they are inclined to take "less crap" than older workers. They are not as automatically loyal to the organization as their fathers, and they are far more cognizant of their own needs and rights. Nor are they as awed by organizational and hierarchical authority. Being less fearful of "discipline" and the threat of losing their jobs, they feel free to express their discontent in myriad ways from fooling around on the job to sabotage. They are better educated than their parents, even without a college degree. They want more freedom and opportunity and will struggle hard to achieve it.

These attitudes suggest that contemporary youth are interested in both meaningful and fulfilling work, a trend confirmed by a 1972 survey of college seniors:

> In work attitudes and perceptions of the most salient characteristics of work, students see themselves as being quite different from their parents. Two significant and striking differences emerge when students are asked to compare their work needs with those of their fathers. Students see themselves as being far less concerned with the nature and purposes of the work. Students stress the more altruistic and intrinsic aspects of the job. They seek interesting work which will be useful to society and of benefit to others, will allow them to express individuality, and will enhance individual growth. [U.S., Department of Labor, Manpower Administration 1974, p. 4]

These studies indicate that today's youth seem less concerned with the pecuniary aspects of jobs and more concerned with the nonpecuniary aspects.[4] This notion is confirmed by a survey of the occupational aspirations of seniors in the high school class of 1972. Fully 54 percent of these students indicated aspirations for professional

TABLE 1

Occupational Aspirations of High School Class of 1972 during Their
Senior Year and Two and One-Half Years Later and Composition of
the Labor Force by Occupation Group, 1972 and 1985

	Percentage Distribution			
	Occupational Aspirations of High School Class of 1972[a]		Labor Force	
			1972	1985
Occupation Group	1972	1974[b]	Actual	Projected
Professional and technical workers	54.0	49.9	14.1	16.8
Clerical workers	16.0	12.7	17.4	19.4
Managers	5.0	11.7	9.8	10.3
Service workers	7.0	4.9	13.5	13.2
Sales workers	3.0	1.9	6.6	6.4
Crafts workers	8.0	9.6	13.2	13.2
Operatives	2.0	4.0	16.5	15.1
Laborers and farm workers	4.0	5.3	8.9	6.0
Total	100.0	100.0	100.0	100.0

[a]Based on responses to questions asking what kind of work respondents would like to do (1972), and what kind of work they expect
to be doing when they are 30 years old (1974).
[b]Preliminary data. Estimates are unweighted.

Note: Percentage distributions may not add to 100.0 because
of rounding.

Source: Golladay (1976), p. 245.

and technical employment (see Table 1). It is predominantly in the
professional, technical, and managerial occupations where one observes the highest degree of both intrinsic and extrinsic rewards
(Bielby and Kalleberg 1975).
　　Recent evidence also indicates that there may be a growing discrepancy between the aspirations and expectations of contemporary
youth, and the availability of jobs that may satisfy them. Table 1

TABLE 2

Distribution of Employment by Occupation Group for Employed
College Graduates, 1966, 1972, and 1978

| Sex and Occupation Group | All[a] | | New Entrants[b] |
	1966	1978	1972
Males			
Professional and technical workers	60.6	52.1	57.3
Managers and administrators	22.7	24.5	13.8
Sales workers	6.8	8.9	7.4
Clerical workers	4.4	4.7	5.4
All other groups	5.5	9.9	16.0
Total	100.0	100.0	100.0
Females			
Professional and technical workers	81.1	65.0	71.5
Managers and administrators	4.1	8.7	5.7
Sales workers	1.2	4.6	3.8
Clerical workers	10.6	15.4	13.7
All other groups	3.0	6.2	5.3
Total	100.0	100.0	100.0

[a]Employed persons 16 years old and over who completed four or more years of college.

[b]Employed persons 16 years old and over who received degrees between July 1971 and June 1972, were in the civilian noninstitutional population, and were not enrolled full time in a college or university as of October 1972.

Note: Percentage distributions may not add up to 100.0 because of rounding.

Source: U.S., Bureau of Labor Statistics 1979a, p. 58; 1974a, p. 34.

also shows the actual and projected distribution of jobs in the U.S. economy suggesting a discrepancy between the occupational aspirations of today's youth and the kinds of jobs they can expect to find upon completing school. Yankelovich also points out the growing disparity between the higher expectations of young people and the lack of opportunity to satisfy them (1974, p. 37). Recent evidence shows that a growing number of college graduates, including recent graduates, are now being employed outside of professional and managerial occupations (Table 2).

The discrepancy between attitudes, expectations, and aspirations, on the one hand, and actual job opportunities, on the other, suggests, although it does not prove, that unrealized expectations may be a worthwhile index of overeducation. For example, a survey of recent college graduates found that one-third of the graduates were employed outside their field of study; of those, two-thirds earned less than they had expected (U.S., Bureau of Labor Statistics 1974a, p. 40). Even one-third of those employed in areas related to their field of study earned less than what they had expected.

To summarize, it seems plausible that the expectations of recent young workers may not be realized in the contemporary labor market. Unfortunately, there are formidable problems in implementing a systematic study of overeducation based on unrealized expectations.

Underutilization of Educational Skills

The final definition of overeducation is based upon the utilization of educationally developed skills within the labor market.

Definition 3: Overeducation exists for those individuals in the labor force who are employed in jobs that do not make full use of their education.

This definition is derived from the popular notion that employers hire persons with particular skills, abilities, and attributes that they feel are necessary to perform efficiently in particular job settings. More simply, every job in the labor market may require a minimum set of worker characteristics. One primarily acquires general skills and abilities from formal training in schools. Contrasting the skill requirements of jobs and skill attainments of workers in those jobs leads to another measure of overeducation: individuals whose educational skills exceed those required to perform their jobs adequately. This assumes that excess skills are not utilized by employers. As the discussion in the next chapter illustrates, there are sound, theoretical reasons that this might be true.

As with previous definitions, this one lends itself to either an individual or social measure of overeducation. It is most apparently an individual measure since it requires an evaluation of each worker's educational qualifications and respective job requirements. As in the preceding definition, an aggregation of those overeducated workers presents a social index of overeducation.

There are several conceptual advantages to this definition. As a gauge of social value or usefulness, it measures directly the utilization of educational skills for each worker in the labor market. In orthodox views of the labor market, earnings directly reflect a worker's contribution to the labor process. But earnings may vary over time with changes in the relative supply and demand of workers. Although the supply and demand for educated workers will also affect the jobs in which they are employed and thus the utilization of their skills, this measure remains a more direct index of whether skills are utilized in the labor market. In addition, social investment in education is often justified by the contribution it makes to the economy, not necessarily in terms of dollars, but simply in terms of supplying skilled workers to the labor market. Individually, workers attach importance to using the skills and abilities they acquired in school. Thus this definition of overeducation is appealing from both an individual and social perspective.

This definition also has disadvantages. Conceptually, it restricts itself to one particular outcome of education—an array of cognitive skills and abilities. From an individual's perspective this may be the most important outcome within the labor market. But from a social perspective, it may be narrow. For example, both the economic system and society in general benefit from the contribution the educational sector makes to the advancement of knowledge.

Methodologically, measuring a discrepancy in skills presents problems. First, it requires that the skill requirements of every job be determined. One difficulty in doing this is differentiating between the general skill requirements of a job and its specific skill requirements (Becker 1975). Job-specific skills are usually acquired through on-the-job training, while only the general skills required for jobs are acquired through schooling. The second methodological problem is that of assessing the general skills of workers. Most individual survey data only contain a worker's educational attainment. Somehow educational attainment must be translated into similarly defined skill requirements of jobs. In summary, although there is definite intuitive appeal to this notion of overeducation, there are formidable problems in evaluating it.

Nonetheless, several studies have examined the utilization of educational skills within the workplace. Some critics have argued that the number of college graduates exceeded the number of jobs requiring a college education as far back as 1950 (Berg 1970). More recently, over one-third of the employed adult population in 1977 reported having skills that were not used in their present jobs (Staines and Quinn 1979). Surveys of college graduates indicate that many find themselves in jobs that do not use all the skills they acquired in college, especially those employed outside their major field of study (U.S., Bureau of Labor Statistics 1974a; Bisconti and Solmon 1976).

Several studies have contrasted the educational attainments of the labor force with information on skill requirements as compiled by the Department of Labor in the Dictionary of Occupational Titles. Rawlins and Ulman (1974) studied workers in selected professional occupations between 1950 and 1960 and concluded "that much of the growth of education in the post-war periods cannot be explained by job-related demand for academic skills" (p. 208). Miller (1971) performed similar analyses using labor market information on workers in October 1966 and concluded the following:

> Preliminary examination of the educational requirements for occupations, on the one hand, and the educational attainment of workers on the other, shows very little similarity. Exceptions are the professional, technical and managerial, farming and machine trades occupations. Apart from these groups, generally considerably less than half of workers were in jobs that require anything more than an elementary education, according to the DOT [Dictionary of Occupational Titles] classification. Nevertheless, well over half of those in every occupational category had at least some high school. Despite the limitations of the data, it is hard to escape the conclusion that the reported high level of education of the American labor force reflects not occupational requirements but a broader set of social values. [P. 3]

Lucas (1972), using data similar to Miller's, observed a "credential effect"; according to this criterion persons are more likely to become overeducated the more schooling they acquire, although persons with two years of college are more likely to become overeducated than persons with four years of schooling (p. 188). Berg, Freedman, and Freeman (1978) observed increasing mismatches between the educational attainments of the labor force and the skill requirements of their jobs from 1950 to 1970.

In summary, there is intuitive appeal in defining overeducation as the discrepancy between the educational skills of the work force and the skill requirements of their jobs. Furthermore, there is some evidence that suggests overeducation may exist in the labor market based on such a definition. Yet, to get an accurate picture of overeducation defined in this manner requires that a number of methodological difficulties be overcome. The discussion in the next chapter points out that the conceptual basis of this definition challenges some basic assumptions of neoclassical economic theory.

SUMMARY

Overeducation in the labor market can be defined in a number of ways. This chapter explored three definitions. Of course, the definitions may overlap. For example, the first definition is based on actual earnings while the second is based on expectations about jobs. The latter could include earnings as one component. The second definition, which deals with expectations, is the most general since it could encompass a number of labor market phenomena associated with education. The first two deal with rewards (for example, earnings, status) associated with educational attainment while the third deals directly with the utilization of cognitive skills. Because the three definitions are based on different labor market phenomena, it is possible to observe the existence of overeducation according to one definition but not another. Recent evidence indicates, however, that overeducation may now exist in the contemporary labor market according to all three definitions (Freeman 1976; U.S., Bureau of Labor Statistics 1974a; Rumberger 1980). Since none of the evidence is conclusive, the problem of selecting the appropriate definition remains. Consequently, except in the empirical section, the discussion of overeducation in this study is not restricted to any single definition.

Chapter 2 concludes the first part of the study by exploring the theoretical foundations of overeducation based on all the definitions presented in this chapter. The second part of the study provides an empirical evaluation of overeducation based on one definition: the discrepancy between the educational attainments of workers and the skill requirements of their jobs. The final part, again using all definitions, explores the implications of overeducation for the workplace as well as for private and public policy.

NOTES

1. The percentage of workers employed in white-collar occupations increased from 31.1 in 1940 to 48.8 in 1974, while the percentage of workers employed in blue-collar occupations decreased from 39.8 in 1940 to 34.3 in 1974. See U.S., Department of Labor (1976), p. 387. The white-collar heading includes professional and

technical workers, managers and administrators except farm, sales, and clerical workers. The blue-collar heading includes craft and kindred workers, operatives, and nonfarm laborers. See U.S., Bureau of the Census (1972) for a complete list of the occupations in each category. Major occupation categories, especially white-collar and blue-collar, bear little resemblance to actual status, work performed, or any other indicative features of jobs. This will be discussed further in Part II.

2. Examples appear in Time (1976), Sheils et al. (1976), Shaffer (1976), and Goodman (1980).

3. The quotation marks, which have heretofore indicated the lack of a widely acknowledged definition of the term overeducation, will now be dropped. But the issue of a suitable definition should remain in the mind of the reader.

4. Flanagan, Strauss, and Ulman (1974) construct a model of labor market preferences that shows how workers' demands for nonpecuniary rewards from their jobs may increase as their pecuniary rewards increase.

2

THEORETICAL EXPLANATIONS
OF OVEREDUCATION

INTRODUCTION

The previous chapter reviewed several ways in which overeducation could exist in the contemporary labor market. Regardless of which definition one chooses, the study of this phenomenon raises the important question, How can overeducation be explained by different theories of the labor market? This chapter will attempt to answer that question.

It is helpful to divide the question into a number of related questions. In order to examine the condition of overeducation, one must consider both the demand and supply of educated labor within the market. First, what are the factors that determine the demand for educated labor? How is education used in production? Most important, what are the criteria for substitution between various categories of educated labor? Second, what are the factors that determine the supply of educated labor into the market? To what degree do the factors that determine supply operate independently from considerations of the market, such as relative wages? Finally, how do supply and demand interact in the market? What determines the relative prices (wages) associated with various categories of educated labor? These questions will form the basis for the forthcoming discussion.

I preface this task by acknowledging the existence of several, often competing, perspectives on the operation of the labor market. They differ with respect to their assumptions, their world views, the aspects of the labor market that they address and, of course, their diagnoses and prognoses about overeducation. The models can be grouped into two categories—orthodox and heterodox. For the most part the orthodox perspectives differ in their explanation of certain aspects of the labor market but share a common foundation; they deal with the actions of individuals and firms in the competitive market and their reactions to various labor market conditions. The heterodox perspectives also deal with different aspects of the labor market yet share a common foundation quite at odds with that of the orthodox views: they focus on the actions of workers and employers as classes or groups rather than as individuals acting independently.

The distinctions between the various models are not meant to disguise any commonality. The motive is simply didactical. As such, a condition of overeducation could be consistent with more than one perspective. The perspectives differ in their explanations of overeducation and in the definitions of overeducation that they recognize; not all models would recognize overeducation according to all three definitions. In fact, not every model would even recognize a condition referred to as overeducation. The intent of this chapter is to explore what each view does have to say. At times this must be inferred, since proponents of each theory have not always explicitly addressed themselves to this phenomenon.

ORTHODOX MODELS OF THE LABOR MARKET

The three orthodox perspectives are human capital, theory screening, and job competition. Human capital theory, a derivative of neoclassical economic theory, is the dominant view of the labor market today. As such, it influences government policy and forms the basis for most current research on the topic. Screening and job competition are actually modifications of certain aspects of the human capital view that share several common premises.

Human Capital

The concept of human capital was developed largely in the work of Schultz (1961) and Becker (1975). In this concept skills and other abilities are considered units of <u>human capital</u>, a term analogous to physical capital in the neoclassical view of the firm (an organized unit of business). Firms no longer simply employ capital and labor, but rather, physical and human capital. Employment decisions are made similarly for both physical and human capital; quantities of each are hired until the value of the marginal product associated with each factor equals the prevailing price or wage. The only major difference between physical and human capital is that human capital is embodied in individuals. Rather than purchasing a quantity of human capital in the market, a firm hires individuals possessing given amounts of human capital. The labor supplied in the market comes in the form of labor services provided by individuals differentiated by their respective embodiments of human capital. The firm then must decide how many of each type of worker to hire. The decision is based on the relative prices (wages) associated with each type of worker as well as their respective marginal productivities.

Probably the least understood component of this theory revolves around the question of the elasticity of substitution among different categories of skilled (educated) labor. An individual firm responds to the relative price differences it must pay for each unit of educated labor (such as college graduates and high school graduates). Hiring decisions are based on the perceived contribution each additional unit of labor makes to production (marginal product). In general, education is hired as a factor of production up until the point where the marginal proportionate increase in efficiency (value added to the firm's output) with respect to education equals the marginal proportionate increase in wages paid to acquire that amount of education (Johnson 1970, p. 191).[1] Exactly how does marginal productivity vary with education? In general, it is claimed that education is positively correlated with marginal productivity and thus rewarded correspondingly with higher wages. Several explanations have been offered to account for this. Welch (1970) suggests that there is an <u>allocative effect</u> to education, meaning that "increased education may enhance a worker's ability to acquire and decode information about costs and productive characteristics of other inputs" (p. 42). Schultz (1975) argues that education enhances a worker's "ability to deal with disequilibria." Similar arguments state that education is complementary to other inputs (capital) and thus the marginal productivity of more-educated labor relative to less-educated labor rises as the amount of capital employed by the firm rises (Nelson and Phelps 1966; Griliches 1969; Welch 1970). Few of these tenets have been tested empirically, except in the case of agriculture. The problem of determining the elasticity of substitution between categories of skilled labor thus remains.

Supply of educated labor (human capital) to the market is predicated on the observed earnings differences between persons of differing educational attainments. In human capital theory, education is undertaken, in part, as an investment activity that produces human capital in persons who go to school. There are costs associated with this activity (both direct and indirect) and expected returns (both pecuniary and nonpecuniary). It is assumed that individuals, as a result of their own tastes and preferences for present and future rewards, with ready access to investment funds, and with perfect knowledge of the market, choose rationally to invest in education such that the expected returns equal the expected costs incurred by such investment (Cohn 1975).

Schooling is only one investment activity that produces human capital. It is also acquired from on-the-job activities, both formal on-the-job training programs and general experience or learning by doing (Becker 1975; Mincer 1974). Some proponents of this viewpoint even suggest that human capital is produced within the family (Chiswick 1973). Not all investment activities take place prior to entering the labor market. More elaborate models examine investment behavior at different stages in a worker's career, using the difference between the expected costs and benefits at each stage (Rosen 1972; Ben-Porath 1967). In this expanded view, firms offer jobs with greater or fewer training opportunities. The relationship between wages and marginal productivity becomes more complicated in this case because the costs of training and returns to training enter into the offered wage. Wages in the investment period reflect marginal productivities as well as costs of training; wages in later years reflect true marginal productivities net of returns to investment in training.

A further complication arises from the mix of human capital between general and specific skills (Becker 1975). General skills are rewarded equally by all firms in the market while specific skills only increase the productivity of an individual within a particular firm. Observed differences in earnings actually reflect differences in the mix of specific and general skills within the human capital stock as well as the returns to that stock. In general, firms absorb the costs of specific training if they can capture the benefits; individuals will absorb the costs of general training since they can reap the benefits of that training.

Some forms of training may be specific to certain kinds of activities and not just specific to particular firms. Although schooling is primarily considered general training, part of it may actually be specific to certain jobs. For example, an undergraduate degree in engineering is more valuable in an engineering-related job than any other because it is only in such a job that the training is fully utilized. An engineer employed outside of the profession would not be similarly rewarded because some of the training would be underutilized.

Given this summary of the human capital perspective, what does it have to say about the condition of overeducation? Since human capital theory is based on the neoclassical theory of the firm, overeducation must be considered in terms of relative wages among different categories of educated labor. Prices are regulated in the market owing to the interaction of supply and demand. In this case relative prices and relative supply and demand are important. Based on neoclassical theory, a fall in relative demand or a rise in relative supply could bring about a fall in the relative salaries of more-educated to less-educated labor.

Several economists have argued that an economic downturn such as occurred in the 1970s could cause the relative demand for educated labor to fall. Becker (1975) and Oi (1962) suggest that declines in product demand could produce differential shifts in the demand for skilled labor. Because firms make more investments in specific training for more educated workers, they would be less willing to lay off those workers during an economic downturn in order to minimize their losses from those investments. This could explain the growth in the relative unemployment rates of college-educated to high-school-educated workers during the 1970s (Golladay 1977, p. 221). It could also explain the decline in the growth of wages for younger, less-experienced workers relative to older, more-experienced workers (Grasso 1977; Freeman 1979; Welch 1979). In addition, there has been a decline in the relative growth rates of education-intensive industries, resulting in a decline in the relative demand for educated workers (Freeman 1976; Smith and Welch 1978).

The relative supply of college graduates entering the labor market has increased dramatically in the last 15 years. This has been due to an increase in the college-age population and an increase in the proportion of this population participating in higher education (Freeman 1976, 1979; Grasso 1977). As a result, there has been a dramatic increase in the number of undergraduate and graduate degrees conferred (See Chapter 4, Figure 2).

Finally, Becker (1975) offers an interesting insight into the determination of supply and demand. He argues that different conceptions of wage differentials influence supply and demand (pp. 75-77). Relative demand for educated workers is influenced by the ratio of relative wages, while the supply of educated workers is influenced by absolute differences in wages between groups. "Clearly a secular decline in wage ratios would not be inconsistent with a secular increase in real wage differences if average wages were rising" (p. 76). This may, in fact, have occurred during the last decade.[2]

In summary, human capital theory offers several explanations of the variation in relative prices among categories of educated labor over time. As such, overeducation does not really exist in this conception, at least in terms of a fall in relative wages. Cyclic movements in the economy will naturally lead to changes in relative prices. Faith is simply put in the market mechanism to regulate these prices. Changes in relative prices will also lead to variations in returns to human capital, although the process becomes complicated by the differences in time when investments are undertaken and returns obtained (Freeman 1971). Thus, the recent declines in the returns to college should not be viewed as a long-term problem. In general, a positive return to investment in human capital will remain as long as the perceived productiveness of human capital generates sufficient returns to justify the costs of such an investment.

Screening

Human capital proponents argue that the observed differences in earnings by persons of different educational attainments can be explained by the different embodiments of human capital. Proponents of screening generally acknowledge that those with more schooling are more productive in the firm and are thus rewarded with higher wages, but they do not attribute these differences to the human capital produced in schools. Rather, they argue that the strong correlation between schooling and earnings is due to the screening function of schools. Persons who acquire more schooling have more ability than those who do not, and it is the ability that is rewarded in the firm. Schooling merely serves as a means of identifying those with more innate ability from those with less. Thus, the relationship between education and earnings explained by human capital proponents is actually misrepresented.

Spence (1973) presents an elaborate model of screening. In his conception, employers must make investment decisions under uncertainty. Employers have little idea about the relative productivity of prospective employees prior to their actual employment. If schooling acts as a signal to identify those individuals who are the most able, then employers offer jobs and wages based on the amount of the signal that individuals possess. After employees begin work, employers observe actual productivity and find that, indeed, persons with more schooling are more productive. Thus, the behavior of employers becomes reinforced as they continue to observe that individuals with more schooling are more productive. In this case, returns to schooling are actually returns to investment in signals. Of course, for schooling to act as a signal, Spence must assume that the costs of schooling vary negatively with ability: more able persons face lower costs of investing in the signal of schooling and therefore acquire more of it. The validity of that assumption is debatable, but the model does offer an explanation of how screening could operate in the labor market.

Screening proponents may not believe that schooling acts exclusively as an investment in information. However, they tend to attribute at least some of the earnings associated with schooling to the information function rather than human capital acquired in school or on the job. Human capital proponents counter such arguments by saying it is only necessary to correct their empirical observations in order to prevent an overstatement of the effect of schooling on earnings. As Mincer (1974) states so emphatically:

However, the question in this study is not what explains earnings, but what are the effects of human capital invest-

ment on earnings. . . . If ability affects earnings only because it affects investment in human capital, one of the
variables is redundant when both are entered in the earnings function. . . . Unless parents' education has an effect on childrens' earnings aside from affecting the investment in their human capital, its inclusion will obscure the
estimated effects of human capital on earnings. [P. 139]

What are the implications of screening theory for overeducation? First, the observation of an educational upgrading of jobs is
consistent with the screening perspective. In the face of an increasing supply of educated labor, employers could raise the minimum entry
requirements on jobs that previously had such requirements and im-
pose minimum entry requirements on jobs that previously had none.
Such actions would most likely affect new entrants into the labor market. For example, employers could require a two-year or four-year
college degree in jobs where ten years ago only a high school diploma
was required.

Screening could also explain variations in the relative earnings
among educated workers. It could limit the supply of workers for
high-paying jobs, resulting in artificially high earnings for persons
holding those jobs (Taubman and Wales 1975, p. 111). An increase in
the supply of persons with educational credentials would subsequently
increase competition for wages in those jobs and thus drive down relative wages. Spence (1973, p. 359) indicates that education may work
as an effective signal only in certain jobs. If all good jobs become
filled by persons having the appropriate signal (educational credentials), the remainder must accept jobs for which their signal is an ineffective indicator of productivity. Thus, as more people with signals
accept employment in those jobs, the average reward to that signal
falls. For instance, a college degree might be a signal of high productivity in many professional jobs, but not in factory jobs. As more
college graduates find employment outside of those areas in which
they traditionally have been employed, the average earnings of all
college graduates may fall relative to less-educated workers.

In addition, if screening does take place, then the social rate-of-
return to educational investments will always be lower than the private
rate, ignoring for a moment differences in cost and benefit measures
used in their calculation (Taubman and Wales 1975, p. 107). Regardless of whether screening occurs, individuals will invest in education
as long as it increases the likelihood of finding employment in high-
paying jobs relative to the costs of investment. But to the degree that
education is used as a screening device, earnings differences between
education groups overstate the true returns to social investment.
Some of those differences are due simply to the income redistribution

effect of credentialism that restricts entry to high-paying jobs and thus artificially maintains high wages (p. 118).

In summary, screening explains the relationship between education and earnings in another way. It attempts to extend human capital theory by accounting for a noneducational factor that influences earnings—ability. But it also leaves some things unexplained. For example, why does education serve as an effective signal for some jobs but not for others? Why do the costs of acquiring education vary by ability?

Job Competition

Thurow (1972, 1974, 1975) has developed a theory of job competition that challenges one of the basic tenets of human capital theory—that earnings are derived from marginal productivities of individuals. He argues that it is theoretically difficult to determine relative marginal productivities between groups of educated workers. Furthermore, his attempts to calculate marginal productivities and elasticities of substitution empirically have led to contradictory and counterintuitive results (1974, pp. 376-81). He also notes that the neoclassical claim of wage competition in the labor market is unsupported by his observation of a wide distribution in the earnings of workers within education categories (pp. 387-89).

Thurow posits that individuals compete in the labor market for jobs and not wages, although he acknowledges that there is probably both job competition and wage competition. In this view, marginal products are associated with jobs and not individuals. Individuals compete for the best jobs based on an array of characteristics that suggest to the employer the cost of training those individuals in the skills necessary to perform any given job. "Thus the labor market is not primarily a market for matching demands and supplies of different job skills, but a market for matching trainable individuals with training ladders" (p. 391).

The two features of this model that require explanation are the labor queue of trainable individuals and the distribution of jobs and earnings. First, an individual's position in the labor queue is based on perceived training costs:

Training costs are the basic determinants of the rank order in the labor queue, but lacking direct evidence on specific training costs for specific workers, laborers are ranked according to their background characteristics—age, sex, educational attainment, previous skills, psychological test, etc. Each is used as an indirect measure of the costs nec-

essary to produce some standard work performance.
[P. 393]

Discrimination becomes possible because subjective elements may
enter into the positioning of people in the queue. Once the labor queue
is established, the best jobs are allocated to the people in the highest
position in the queue and so on until all the jobs are filled.

The distribution of jobs and earnings results from three factors:
the character of technical progress, the sociology of wage determination, and the distribution of training costs. Technical progress, as
in neoclassical theory, is assumed to be an exogenous factor that operates to make production more efficient. The second factor arises
from "the distribution of economic power and senses of justice among
workers and employers" that operates on the remainder of the output
not associated with marginal products (p. 401). The third factor re-
ceives the most attention in Thurow's analysis. The distribution of
training costs is governed by background characteristics (such as education) of people in the labor queue. A shift in the distribution of education changes the distribution of training costs and ultimately the
distribution of earnings. Education actually serves two functions. It
determines one's relative position in the labor queue and consequently
one's job and potential earnings, and it affects the training costs and
thus the maximum amount one can earn from a given job (since observed earnings differences are net of training costs). The sharing
of training costs between employer and employee complicates the analysis, but does not alter the basic operation of the model.

The job competition model offers several insights into overeducation and the effects of changes in the distribution of educated labor
supplied to the market. In general, more-educated workers always
earn more than less-educated workers. An increase in the supply of
college-educated workers, for example, simply results in their re-
placing workers with less than a college education. As a result, the
private incentive to invest in schooling will remain as long as those
relative advantages continue and outweigh the costs of investment.
It may even be necessary for individuals to acquire more education
over time simply to maintain their relative position in the labor queue.
The dynamics of this model also predict an educational upgrading of
jobs in the face of increases in the supply of educated labor. For
these reasons, the model predicts a divergence between social and
private rates-of-return.

In job competition, differences in earnings among various
groups of educated workers depend upon the relative supplies of educated labor. "According to a job-competition model, the most preferred group (college workers) would have experienced an equaliza-
tion of income within their group, a rise in income relative to other

groups, but a fall in income relative to the national average" (p. 409). Thurow presents evidence from 1950-70 that substantiates those predictions.

In Thurow's model, overeducation does not exist in terms of relative salaries, but in terms of occupational position. The model provides a plausible explanation of why the relative earnings of college graduates may never subside appreciably. But the model fails to explain fully the three factors that determine the distribution of earnings and jobs as well as their interaction. Perhaps the largest unexplained part of the model is the elasticity of training costs with respect to education and the size of those training costs (p. 407). Thurow acknowledges these factors but fails to explain them in detail. Nonetheless, the model does offer an intuitively appealing interpretation of the phenomenon of overeducation.

HETERODOX VIEWS OF THE LABOR MARKET

The orthodox views that were just discussed have two elements in common. First, they examine labor market activity from an individual perspective; individual workers enter the labor market with a given set of traits and educational credentials in search of suitable employment, and individual employers or firms seek labor of differing qualities to fill their own needs. The labor market situation is merely a composite of individual activity. Each participant in the market undertakes investment activities, in the former case dictated by utility maximization and in the latter case dictated by profit maximization. Second, orthodox theories are essentially ahistorical. They deal largely with how the market functions given a supply and demand for educated labor. The theories deal with the formation of supply and demand only insofar as they are influenced by the market situation, such as the relative wages paid to various categories of educated labor. Other forces, including those that influence the formation of individual tastes and preferences or those that influence the development of technology, lie outside the theoretical domain.

Heterodox approaches, on the other hand, examine labor market activity through an analysis of groups or classes of individuals. They are usually historical in nature. Proponents of heterodox perspectives observe the labor market not as a composite of individual actions or activities, but rather, as groups of individuals who face similar labor market situations and develop similar tastes and preferences (Bowles and Gintis 1976, p. 67). Heterodox perspectives also address a wider range of factors that orthodox models take as exogenous; for example, heterodox theories consider technology and its influence on the demand for various kinds of labor over time. In this way heterodox models are more "robust," although their complexity also makes them more difficult to prove empirically.

This section examines two heterodox perspectives—labor market segmentation and a radical view. As in the case of the orthodox perspectives, there is considerable overlap between these two views. For the sake of discussion, however, the basic tenets of each and their implications for overeducation will be examined separately.

Labor Market Segmentation

Labor market segmentation presents a relatively recent challenge to orthodox views of the labor market. This view arose from attempts to explain a wide variety of economic phenomena that its proponents claim are left largely unexplained by conventional theories, including the persistence of poverty, income inequality, discrimination, and unemployment (Cain 1976). In contrast to orthodox views of the labor market, segmented labor market (SLM) perspectives divide the labor market into distinct segments that function differently from each other and in which certain groups of workers are concentrated.

There is little consensus among SLM proponents as to just how the labor market is stratified. Most work has focused on divisions of jobs or occupations. Doeringer and Piore (1971, pp. 1-2) suggest two divisions, one of which is referred to as

> the internal labor market, an administrative unit, such as a manufacturing plant, within which the pricing and allocation of labor is governed by a set of administrative rules and procedures. The internal labor market, governed by administrative rules, is to be distinguished from the external labor market of conventional economic theory where pricing, allocating, and training decisions are governed directly by economic variables. These two markets are interconnected, however, and movement between them occurs at certain job classifications which constitute ports of entry and exit to and from the internal labor market. The remainder of jobs within the internal market are filled by the promotion or transfer of workers who have already gained entry to it. Consequently, these jobs are shielded from the direct influences of competitive forces in the external labor market.

Occupations that are subject to the dynamics of the internal labor market constitute the primary segment; remaining jobs compose the secondary segment. Other SLM proponents have suggested that the labor

market actually consists of three or more distinct occupational segments (Reich, Gordon, and Edwards 1973; Carter and Carnoy 1974;
Harrison 1972; Freedman and Maclachan 1976). Attention has also
focused on industrial divisions of the labor market (Beck, Horan,
and Tolbert II 1978; D'Amico 1978). Finally, new variants of the
SLM perspective attempt to combine occupational and industrial divisions into one, more complete, notion of segmentation (Edwards 1979;
Carnoy 1980; Levin et al forthcoming).

There are a number of basic propositions posited by SLM advocates. First, certain race and sex groups have historically been concentrated in certain segments. For example, women and minorities
are concentrated in the lowest or secondary segment. Second, not
only are earnings higher in some segments than others, but the manner in which wages are determined varies from segment to segment.
Cognitive traits are treated differently in different segments and af-
fective traits necessary for participation in the segments are different.
This means that investment in schooling or other forms of training
may lead to higher wages in some segments than in others. Third,
mobility between segments is restricted; once an individual enters
one of the segments it is often very difficult to gain access to another.
Jobs in the highest segments that operate with internal labor markets
are filled primarily with other workers from that same segment.
Finally, segments vary with respect to employment security with the
lower segments characterized by higher unemployment rates.

Aside from differences among SLM proponents on the number of
actual segments that exist in the labor market, there is a division between those who argue for its existence along essentially neoclassical
lines and those who offer a radical or Marxist interpretation. Piore
(1973; 1975) falls in the first group; Reich, Gordon, and Edwards
(1973) represent the second group. Piore (1975, pp. 140-43), for
example, argues that segmentation arose from technological considerations and the nature of product demand. He also argues that the supply of labor into different segments is due, in part, to class subcul-
tures that inculcate different tastes and traits making some workers
suitable for employment in only certain segments. Reich, Gordon,
and Edwards, in contrast, argue that factors of workers' tastes and
the evolution of technology result from the dominating influence of
capitalists and capitalist production in all aspects of society. Technology is not neutral in their scheme, but is utilized in special ways
by capitalists to further the development of capitalism. Moreover,
capitalists, in order to further their own class interests, engage in
efforts to structure the internal relations of the firm, which would
break down unified worker interests (1973, pp. 361-63). These activities include the exploitation of racial and ethnic groups.

Segmentation theory is a relatively recent development and has
yet to be fully delineated. But efforts have been made to test empiri-

cally some of its basic tenets (Osterman 1975; Harrison 1972; Rumberger and Carnoy 1980). Enough interest has been generated to elicit criticisms from advocates of the neoclassical perspective (Cain 1976; Wachter 1974). Thus, it is worthwhile to consider what this theory implies about overeducation.

First, the existence of internal labor markets, protected from external market forces, suggests that an increase in the supply of educated workers may not bring about a better utilization of those workers. That is, relative supplies may do little to affect relative wages in internal labor markets. In the higher or primary segments, education may serve as a screen into entry-level jobs. Once those jobs are filled by educationally qualified individuals, the remainder must fill lower-level jobs. Since different segments reward worker traits differently, there is little reason to believe that educationally implanted skills and traits will be utilized in the lower segments. In fact, education may serve no useful purpose in these segments. Workers in this situation face restricted entry into higher segments, leaving the option of quitting and going to another firm.

Segmentation theory also suggests that the condition of overeducation may exist as much in low-level segments as in upper-level segments. Workers with only moderate levels of education (such as high school completion) may be overeducated because they are employed in jobs where education is unrewarded and unnecessary to perform the tasks of those jobs. This is why SLM proponents have repeatedly argued that government policies designed to better the condition of the poor and disadvantaged in this country through educational opportunity may have little effect as long as those workers are restricted to jobs that make little use of such training. To better the lot of these workers, as well as that of recent college graduates employed in low-level jobs, will require a change in utilization of these workers within the firms where they are employed.

Labor market segmentation is an incomplete theory; it does not attempt to explain all aspects of labor market activity. It does, however, offer potentially useful insights into the demand and utilization of labor within the market.

A Radical Perspective

By and large, the aforementioned labor market theories consider the demand and supply of educated labor independently of one another. Orthodox perspectives leave the formation of demand to the unexplained influence of technology. The formation of supply is attributed partially to the unexplained factors of individual tastes and preferences. Supply and demand only interact through the market, with the resulting determination of relative wages. Individuals simply respond to these relative prices given their tastes; firms respond given their technology. Screening and job competition amend some of these processes, yet remain focused on the market mechanism and the independent formulation of supply and demand. Except for the radical formulation of labor market segmentation, all of these models argue that separate forces influence the formation of supply and demand.

A radical view of the labor market, in contrast, necessarily enjoins all factors that influence both supply and demand.[3] This results from its Marxist tradition, one that places primary emphasis on the economic structure as the driving force of the entire society. All social institutions, including schools, operate under the dominating influence of the economic structure. In the case of the United States, the economic system is that of corporate capitalism. In order to understand the functioning of the labor market and education within a radical framework, several characteristics of corporate capitalism require elaboration.

Of primary importance in a radical perspective is the concept of wage labor. A capitalist system is characterized by private ownership of the means of production. These owners (capitalists) or their appointed representatives (high-level managers) have full control over the production process. Workers sell their labor power (capacity to perform work) to these firms in exchange for a wage. It is up to the capitalists to extract as much labor as possible from the worker during the contracted period of employment.[4] The majority of workers today are employed as wage laborers, with a high percentage employed in large, bureaucratic firms (U.S., Department of Health, Education and Welfare 1973, p. 21).

Radicals explain the division of labor in the economy and the demand for labor within the context of the wage-labor system. They argue that capitalists have complete control over the production process. Capitalists seek to perpetuate their class interests through the accumulation of capital and, subsequently, through the growth of their wealth and power. Braverman (1974) examines how the production process under capitalism takes on a unique form—a division of labor where control of the production process is taken over from the worker by the capitalists and where production tasks are divided into simple, routine parts performed by different workers.

> That the first step breaks up only the process, while the
> second dismembers the worker as well, means nothing
> to the capitalist, and all the less since, in destroying
> the craft as a process under the control of the workers,
> he reconstitutes it as a process under his own control.
> He can now count his gains in a double sense, not only

> in productivity but in management control, since that which
> mortally injures the worker is in this case advantageous
> to him. [P. 78]

This process fragmentizes job tasks into their respective parts.[5] It
means that lower-skilled workers can be employed at lower wages in
the most simple operations, reserving the employment of more-
skilled workers for only a few operations. Technology, as employed
by capitalists, furthers this process and lessens the need for skilled
labor. Thus, the development of job hierarchies came about not as
a result of inevitable technical development but through the conscious
efforts of capitalists to further their control over the production process and increase the extraction of a labor surplus (Marglin 1974).
Both technical efficiency and control, therefore, account for the hierarchical division of labor.

In the capitalist division of labor, social relations of production
are as important as the technical relations. Labor is put in a contradictory and alienating situation (Ollman 1971). The capitalist requires the use of labor power in production, yet controls the product
and the means of production. The laborer has little motivation to
work hard under these circumstances. Given the characteristics of
work under capitalism, a number of worker traits are desired by employers to ensure the effective integration of workers into this system.
They include cognitive capacities and concrete technical skills; personality traits, such as motivation, perseverance, and docility, that
enable the individual to operate effectively in a given work role; modes
of self-presentation, such as manner of speech and dress; ascriptive
characteristics, such as race, sex, and age; and credentials, such
as level and prestige of education (Bowles and Gintis 1976, pp. 94-95).

In summary, the economic inequality found in the United States
is reflected in the unequal position of two classes in society—workers
and capitalists. Capitalists, who control the means of production and
dictate the structure of work, seek two objectives:

> The first is to reproduce their positions of privilege in the
> hierarchy of production. A closely related second objec-
> tive is to secure long-term profits, without which the enter-
> prise would cease to exist. Thus profits are sought as an
> instrument in maintaining their class position as the direc-
> tors of the firm and as their source of income. [P. 81]

In other words, it is important to understand not only the utilization
of labor power within production in the short run but also the intergenerational reproduction of labor power that ensures the perpetua-
tion of the capitalist system and its unequal class positions. It is the
educational system that functions to reproduce labor power.

The educational system operates to prepare individuals to assume the unequal positions of economic life in a number of ways:

First, schooling produces many of the technical and cognitive skills required for adequate job performance. Second, the educational system helps legitimate economic inequality. . . . The objective and meritocratic orientation of U.S. education reduces discontent over both the hierarchical division of labor and the process through which individuals attain position in it. Third, the school produces, rewards, and labels personal characteristics relevant to the staffing of positions in the hierarchy. Fourth, the education system, through the pattern of status distinctions it fosters, reinforces the stratified consciousness on which the fragmentation of subordinate economic classes is based. [Pp. 129-30]

In particular, Bowles and Gintis emphasize the reproduction of unequal social class position through education. They argue that educational attainments are highly correlated with social class background; persons of high social class acquire more education, even controlling for IQ differences among classes. Education is also correlated with income; persons with more education earn more than people with less. Finally, social class background directly influences income, even after controlling for education (pp. 112-13). Thus, there is an intergenerational reproduction of social class position that is, in part, legitimized through the educational system.

The relationship between the school system and the production process is characterized by correspondence. First, there is a structural correspondence between the organization of schools and work reflected in similar patterns of hierarchy, patterns of authority, and bureaucracy (Levin 1980a). Second, there is a replication of the social relations of production in the social relations of the school. "It also embraces the content of work and schooling processes such that the combination of form and content of schooling processes tend to support the existing social relations of work, to reconcile children to the ultimate occupational positions that they will occupy within the work structure and to prepare them for the duties that will be associated with those positions" (p. 149). Correspondence arises from the centrality of the economic system and its influence on the political process and the unconscious actions of individual students, parents, teachers, and administrators (Bowles and Gintis 1976; Levin 1980a; Levin et al., forthcoming).

But the principle of correspondence does not completely explain the development and functioning of the schools. The production process changes over time placing new requirements on the schools, in part, in response to the internal contractions of the work process itself.

> We are suggesting that the relationship between education
> and work is a dialectical one. While the influence of the
> work structure has exerted constant pressures to maintain
> a corresponding educational structure for reproducing
> labor power for the capitalist mode of production, the edu-
> cational system also has its own semi-autonomous dynamic
> which causes it to diverge in certain respects from the over-
> all pattern of correspondence and mediation of the internal
> contradictions of capitalist production. At some point this
> divergence will trigger or exacerbate the manifestations of
> the contradictions in production, with deleterious conse-
> quences for the further expansion of production and the re-
> production of existing relations. At that point, both the
> education and production systems will be characterized by
> "reforms" which will attempt to mediate the contradictions
> through alterations in the nature of work relationships and
> corresponding modifications in education. [Levin 1980a,
> pp. 155-56]

Thus, the relationship between the educational system and the production system is at the same time one of correspondence and contradic-
tion. Both systems are in a constant state of change, which these principles attempt to explain. [6]
   Overeducation can be viewed in two ways from this perspective.
First, an overeducated work force (in terms of overqualified workers)
may reflect part of a reserve army of labor. A reserve army of
labor serves two functions. It constitutes a ready supply of labor
that can be drawn into the active work force as needed, such as during times of expansionary activity, and it serves as a means of controlling the active work force by putting downward pressure on wages
—thereby increasing capitalists' surplus and giving capitalist employers the power of threatened dismissal (Baran 1957). The oversupply
of skilled workers in the labor force may have functional importance
in the capitalist system.

> At most levels in the occupational hierarchy mental skills
> are productive, but are not scarce, and hence do not bear
> a direct monetary return. Indeed, we have suggested that
> the educational system serves to produce surpluses of
> skilled labor, thereby increasing the power of employers
> over workers. [Bowles and Gintis 1976, p. 114]

In addition, relative wages reflect neither relative productivities in the workplace nor the relative supplies of skilled workers in the labor force. Relative wages between workers of different educational attainments naturally vary in this scheme because of ongoing class struggles between workers and capitalists, different arrangements for control and exploitation among capitalists, and the uneven development of capitalism.

There is another way of viewing the phenomenon of overeducation based on the principles of correspondence and the independent dynamic of schooling. It accounts for the apparent divergence between supply and demand for educated labor that has occurred in the last decade. To a large degree the rapid expansion of the higher education system in the 1960s can be attributed to the rapid expansion of those industries and occupations requiring highly skilled labor. During this period the educational system was corresponding to the needs of capitalist production. But as suggested earlier, the educational system is also guided by a semiautonomous dynamic. For example, there was increasing political pressure during this period for an increase in educational opportunities for previously excluded groups, especially blacks. The increase in governmental support of educational programs was partly a response to this pressure. As long as the economy was expanding there was no conflict between the growth of the educational system and the needs of capitalist production.

But the economic downturn that began in 1970 suddenly reduced the need for educated workers. Thus, the educational and production systems diverged. This divergence has led to reforms in both the schools and the workplaces in an attempt to reestablish correspondence (Levin 1980a; Levin et al. forthcoming). Examples include recent attempts to reorganize work in response to the larger numbers of educated workers in the labor force. There are also reforms occurring in the educational system. For example, much of the growth in higher education has occurred at the community college level, with social relations corresponding to middle levels of the occupational hierarchy (Karabel 1972). These kinds of changes will continue in an attempt to bring the functioning of schools more nearly in line with the needs of capitalist production.

In summary, the condition of overeducation can be seen, in one way, as functional for maintaining capitalist production and, in another, as arising accidentally from the semiautonomous dynamics of the educational system and the workplace. The domain of analysis incorporated in a radical perspective makes it difficult to test in the same manner as orthodox models. It does attempt, though, to provide a systematic understanding of the functioning of schools and their relationship to the capitalist economic system.

SUMMARY AND CONCLUSION

The perspectives presented in this chapter are based on different assumptions and tenets. They also focus on different aspects of the labor market. [7] As such, each presents a different interpretation of how overeducation could come about, what it means, and what are the likely labor market adjustments to the situation.

The human capital model views education as a major producer of human capital, a scarce commodity used within the firm. The market regulates the relative supply and demand for categories of educated labor given the existence of other exogenous factors such as tastes and technology. Through the functioning of the market, relative supply and demand both respond to relative prices (wages) as well as interact to produce those relative prices. As such, it is consistent within this viewpoint that the wages of college graduates relative to those of high school graduates could fall in response to a relative increase in supply of the former. A decline in relative wages could also result from a relative decrease in demand for educated workers. The educational upgrading of jobs could be a sign of increased skill requirements. What is left unexplained is how workers can possess more skills than their jobs require.

The screening perspective suggests that education serves, in part, as an indicator of the potential productivity of workers for the firm. In this case more education always indicates greater potential productivity. As a result, the educational qualifications of jobs increase in the face of large increases in the supply of highly educated labor as long as employers' costs (additional wages paid) justify such action.

The job competition theory suggests that education also serves as an indicator to the firm, but as an indicator of trainability for a job rather than of individual productivity. In this perspective marginal productivity is associated with jobs and not individuals. The labor market functions as a job queue where potential workers are ranked in a continuum based on employers' perceptions of trainability (as well as other subjective preferences). Education serves as an indicator—more-educated persons occupy higher positions in the job queue than less-educated individuals. The market operates by employers putting the persons at the top of the queue into the best jobs— those with the best pay and other rewards. Workers are then trained in the requisite skills for the jobs that they occupy. In this case the amount of education one has in relation to everyone else becomes important. Thus, there will always be a positive incentive to acquire more education, even in the face of large increases in the supply of educated workers.

Labor market segmentation suggests that there is not a single continuum of jobs in the labor market similarly influenced by the factors of technology and with similar entrance requirements. Rather, segmentation proponents suggest that separate and distinct labor markets exist that are subject to different rules for promotion, have different means of wage determination, and have restricted entry. The forces of competition have little influence within a segmented labor market perspective. Wages, therefore, depend as much on the type of job and segment where one works as on one's educational qualifications. The types of jobs within the various segments also limit the possibilities for utilizing skills. Because of the independent nature of the demand for labor, a condition of overeducation is very conceivable in this perspective.

Finally, a radical perspective suggests that the educational system generally corresponds to the needs of capitalist production. In one sense, overeducation, as an oversupply of skilled workers in the labor market, has functional importance and operates to help the employers control the actions and wages of workers in all levels of the job hierarchy. Overeducation can also arise from a divergence between the schooling system and the economic system as a consequence of their semi-independent dynamics. The uneven nature of capitalist growth suggests that there will always be periods of divergence between the two systems with resulting changes both in the nature of work and in the nature of schools.

The labor market perspectives outlined in this chapter explain overeducation in a variety of ways. They also focus on different meanings of overeducation, with the human capital model dealing mainly with relative prices, while other models address the utilization of skilled labor in firms and wages. Overeducation based on unrealized expectations applies mainly in the radical model.

It was not the intention of this chapter to endorse the labor market perspective that provides the most plausible account of the condition of overeducation. Instead, this review illustrates how the condition of overeducation may be explained by more than one view of the labor market. The choice among perspectives is not based on the evidence alone; it also depends upon the world view that one holds.

The focus of this study now shifts to an empirical examination of overeducation based on one of the definitions outlined in Chapter 1. A discussion of those results and how they relate to the various labor market perspectives will come in the last chapter.

NOTES

1. Firms must actually hire a discrete number of workers with different educational attainments. If there are distinct marginal productivities associated with persons of different educational attainments employed in similar jobs, the possibility of overeducation be-

comes more apparent, as Johnson (1970) points out. In this case the marginal productivity of a highly educated person could actually become negative and there would be a disincentive for employers to replace less-educated workers with more-educated workers. But then the question arises, Why don't employers rearrange production in such a fashion as to use the potentially high productivity of educated workers?

2. Recent research by this author shows that for white males there was a slight decline in the ratio of college to high school earnings between 1969 and 1975, although there was an increase in the absolute earnings differences (Rumberger 1980).

3. There have been many more criticisms of orthodox economic theory by radicals than concrete formulations of the role of education in capitalist society. Therefore, what I refer to as a "radical perspective" is actually a synthesis of Bowles and Gintis (1976) and Levin et al. (forthcoming) and Levin (1980a). It constitutes a radical view but by no means the only possible radical explanation of the role of education in capitalist society.

4. Bowles and Gintis (1976, pp. 95-96) describe the characteristics of the work hierarchy as follows:

> First, the duties, responsibilities, and privileges of individuals are determined neither according to individual preference nor cooperative decision by workers, but rather by a system of formal and informal rules which guide the individual worker's participation in the work process and set limits on his or her actions. Second, the relationships among workers are characterized by hierarchical authority and interdependence. An individual's actions are closely tied to the wills of his or her superiors and the results of these actions have repercussions on large numbers of other workers. Third, while control emanates ultimately from the top, the principle of hierarchical authority implies that middle-level workers have essential, though circumscribed, areas of decision and choice. Fourth, that jobs are determined on the basis not of workers' needs or interests, but rather in the interests of profitability implies that workers cannot be adequately motivated by the intrinsic rewards of the work process.

5. Braverman suggests that the fragmentation of jobs occurs at all levels of the job hierarchy, including white-collar and professional jobs, thus reducing requisite job skills for large numbers of workers over time.

6. For a more general discussion of dialectical analysis see Ollman (1971, chap. 5). Relationships between parts of a social system, such as work and schools, are changing constantly and simultaneously, making it difficult to distinguish "cause" and "effect" (p. 17).

7. For an excellent discussion of three of the labor market perspectives—orthodox, segmented labor markets, and radical—see Gordon (1972).

PART II
EMPIRICAL
INVESTIGATION

3

METHODOLOGY

INTRODUCTION

In the first section of this study overeducation was discussed from a general perspective using several possible definitions. This section investigates the incidence of overeducation based on the third definition that was introduced: the discrepancy between educational attainments of workers and the educational requirements of their jobs. Although overeducation can be measured in several ways, this measure is perhaps the most straightforward. It is commonly believed that education develops cognitive skills and abilities that contribute to the labor process. It is also thought that jobs require different degrees and types of skills. Theoretically, it should be possible to measure any discrepancy that exists between the skills required to perform the tasks of any job and the skills possessed by the worker holding that job. This definition, therefore, attempts to measure directly the utilization of skills in the labor market in contrast to earnings, which only provide an indirect measure of skill utilization.

Constructing this measure of overeducation requires information on both the skill requirements of jobs and the educational attainments of workers. It is also necessary to convert the skill requirements of jobs into equivalent years of schooling in order to compare them with educational attainments. Even with the requisite information, constructing this index presents a number of challenges.

The first concerns the definition of job skill requirements. In this study they are defined as the minimum set of skills required for adequate job performance. Employers require evidence of those skills from prospective applicants in order to ensure that they can perform the tasks of their jobs in a satisfactory manner. There is an important difference between these objective skill requirements and the hiring requirements established by employers (Fine 1968).

45

The former are more likely to be fixed, at least in the short run, while the latter reflect employers' preferences and are more likely to rise as the supply of qualified individuals increases.

A second problem with this approach is determining the skills possessed by workers. This study focuses on general skills, not specific skills. The former are principally acquired in school while the latter can be acquired from a number of sources, including vocational education, on-the-job training, and experience. In this research, measuring overeducation involves contrasting the general educational skills of workers with the skill requirements of their jobs. But information on general skills is rarely available; however, information is commonly available on the number of years of schooling completed by workers. Thus, years of schooling must serve as a proxy for levels of general skills. This assumes that completion of a given level of schooling by one individual represents the same level of general skills as every other worker who has completed that same level. There are many reasons that this assumption is not strictly valid, a matter discussed in the last section of this chapter.

Finally, there is the problem of converting the skill requirements of jobs into equivalent years of schooling. This problem is addressed at greater length in the last section of the chapter. The idea of contrasting differences in educational or skill requirements and educational attainments may be challenged for conceptual reasons as well. While most people may accept the notion of minimum performance requirements, they may not believe that the differences between such requirements and workers' capabilities (as reflected in their educational attainments) constitute an appropriate measure of overeducation.

In particular, such an idea conflicts with the neoclassical idea of human capital and marginal productivity. Recall from Chapter 2 that in the neoclassical view of the firm, education is a primary source of human capital that contributes to the productivity of the individual within the firm. In theory, firms should strive to make efficient use of increases in the education (human capital) of their workers by redesigning jobs or substituting workers with lower skills at lower wages. The idea of workers having more educational skills (human capital) than is required to fulfill the minimum performance requirements of their jobs is therefore inconsistent with profit maximization in the neoclassical framework. Insofar as firms fail to make use of the changing educational attainments (human capital) of their work force, or if marginal productivity is really associated with jobs and not individuals, as Thurow suggests, then the idea of contrasting educational attainments with minimum requirements is a sound one.

One purpose of this research is to investigate whether overeducation is only a recent phenomenon or whether it has existed for some time. This requires information on skill requirements and educational attainments from at least two different points in time. To assess the contemporary situation requires recent information. Since the post-secondary system grew rapidly during the 1960s, a good point for comparison would be sometime in the early part of that decade when overeducation may not have existed. Unfortunately, the availability of appropriate data constrains the choice.

The years 1960 and 1976 were chosen for such a comparison. Fortunately, these two years satisfy the above criteria quite well. The year 1960 marked the beginning of both an economically prosper-ous decade and one of rapid growth of participation in postsecondary education; 1976 marked the beginning of a recovery from a recession-ary period. In fact, 1976 was a time when much of the interest in the idea of overeducation came to the public's attention. It provides a good point with which to assess the contemporary situation.

The remainder of this chapter discusses the methodology of the empirical investigation in detail. The next section describes the sources of data used in this study; the section following outlines how the data sets for the years 1960 and 1976 were constructed. Follow-ing that is a presentation of the empirical procedures used to evaluate the incidence of overeducation in the two years. Finally, the sources of bias and potential error in the estimates are discussed, followed by a brief summary of the chapter.

SOURCES OF DATA

The measure of overeducation used in this study requires infor-mation on the characteristics of jobs (that is, their educational re-quirements) and the characteristics of workers holding those jobs (that is, their educational attainments). Ideally one source of data would contain information on both, and the task of analyzing any dis-crepancies between these two would be easy. Unfortunately, this is not the case. Although the government gathers information on both job characteristics and individual worker characteristics, this information is collected by separate agencies. Specifically, information on work-ers' educational attainments comes from the U.S. Bureau of the Cen-sus; information on the skill requirements of jobs comes from the U.S. Employment Service of the Department of Labor.

Information on Jobs

The U.S. Employment Service periodically collects information on a cross section of jobs in the U.S. labor market. It issues this in-formation in the Dictionary of Occupational Titles (DOT). The infor-

mation is collected by the Employment Service from affiliated State
Employment Service Occupational Analysis Field Centers throughout
the country (U.S., Employment Service 1977, p. xiv). In particular

> The data for the Dictionary were collected and developed
> according to job analysis techniques established by the
> U.S. Employment Service. In most cases, the same job
> was analyzed in two different establishments in one State
> and then in two different establishments in another State.
> The findings of these studies were correlated and job def-
> initions prepared. As a result, information presented in
> the Dictionary reflects the findings of the U.S. Employment
> Service from approximately 75,000 studies of individual job
> situations. Although an occupation was found to have cer-
> tain characteristics in job situations observed by the U.S.
> Employment Service, that does not necessarily preclude
> the same occupation from having different characteristics
> in situations not studied. [U.S., Employment Service
> 1966, p. vii]

The U.S. Employment Service gathers a variety of information on the
characteristics of jobs. First, information is collected on how workers' job tasks relate to data, people, and things (U.S., Employment
Service 1977, pp. xvii-xviii). Second, an array of information is collected on "those abilities, personal traits, and individual characteristics required of a worker in order to achieve average successful
job performance"—referred to as worker traits (U.S., Employment
Service 1965, vol. II, p. 651). Six components of worker traits are
assessed (pp. 651-56):

    1. Training time—the amount of general educational develop-
ment and specific vocational preparation a worker must have.
    2. Aptitudes—the specific capacities and abilities required of
him in order to learn or perform certain tasks or duties.
    3. Interests—preferences for certain types of work activities
or experiences considered necessary for job success.
    4. Temperaments—types of occupational situations to which an
individual must adjust.
    5. Physical demands—physical activities required in work situ-
ation.
    6. Working conditions—physical surroundings prevalent in jobs.

    The DOT contains information on both general training—general
educational development (GED)—and specific training—specific vocational preparation (SVP). This study focuses on the former because
it relates primarily to the training acquired in school. More specifically, GED.

This embraces those aspects of education (formal and in-
formal) which contribute to the worker's (a) reasoning development and ability to follow instructions, and (b) acqui-
sition of "tool" knowledges, such as language and mathe-
matical skills. It is education of a general nature which
does not have a recognized, fairly specific, occupational
objective. Ordinarily such education is obtained in elementary school, high school, or college. It also derives
from experience and individual study. [P. 651]

Table 3 explains the components of the GED scale. Each job may require different levels for each of the three components, although one
would not expect a great variation in the three components for any one
job title.

Specific vocational preparation attempts to measure "the amount
of time required to learn the techniques, acquire information, and develop the facility needed for average performance in a specific job-
worker situation" (p. 652). This training includes (U.S., Department
of Labor 1972, p. 209):

1. Vocational education—high school, commercial or shop
training, technical school, art school, and that part of college training which is organized around a specific vocational objective.

2. Apprenticeship training—training obtained only in those jobs
offering apprenticeships.

3. In-plant training—training given by employer in the form of
organized classroom study.

4. On-the-job training—instruction given to learner or trainee
on the job by a qualified worker.

5. Essential experience in other jobs—experience received in
less responsible jobs or other jobs which qualify for a higher grade
job.

Unlike GED levels, SVP levels are directly translated into specific
units of time (U.S., Employment Service 1965, vol. II, p. 653):

Level	Time
1	Short demonstration only
2	Anything beyond short demonstration up to and including 30 days
3	Over 30 days up to and including 3 months
4	Over 3 months up to and including 6 months
5	Over 6 months up to and including 1 year
6	Over 1 year up to and including 4 years
7	Over 2 years up to and including 4 years
8	Over 4 years up to and including 10 years
9	Over 10 years

TABLE 3

Components of the GED Scale

Level	Reasoning Development	Mathematical Development	Language Development
6	Apply priniciples of logical or scientific thinking to a wide range of intellectual and practical problems. Deal with nonverbal symbolism (formulas, scientific equations, graphs, musical notes, and so on) in its most difficult phases. Deal with a variety of abstract and concrete variables. Apprehend the most abstruse classes of concepts.	Apply knowledge of advanced mathematical and statistical techniques, such as differential and integral calculus, factor analysis, and probability determination, or work with a wide variety of theoretical mathematical concepts and make original applications of procedures, as in empirical and differential equations.	Comprehension and expression of a level to —Report, write, or edit articles for such publications as newspapers, magazines, and technical or scientific journals. Prepare and draw up deeds, leases, wills, mortgages, and contracts. —Prepare and deliver lectures on politics, economics, education, or science. —Interview, counsel, or advise such people as students, clients, or patients, in such matters as welfare eligibility, vocational rehabilitation, mental hygiene, or marital relations. —Evaluate engineering technical data to design buildings and bridges.
5	Apply principles of logical or scientific thinking to define problems, collect data, establish facts, and draw valid conclusions. Interpret an extensive variety of technical instructions, in books, manuals, and mathematical or diagrammatic form. Deal with several abstract and concrete variables.		
4	Apply principles of rational systems* to solve practical problems and deal with a variety of concrete variables in situations where only limited standardization exists. Interpret a variety of in-	Perform ordinary arithmetic, algebraic, and geometric procedures in standard, practical applications.	Comprehension and expression of a level to —Transcribe dictation, make appointments for executive and handle his personal mail, interview and screen people wishing to speak to him, and write routine correspondence on own initiative.

	Reasoning development	Mathematical development	Language development
	... structures furnished in written, oral, diagrammatic, or schedule form.		—Interpret technical manuals as well as drawings and specifications, such as layouts, blueprints, and schematics. —Interview job applicants to determine work best suited for their abilities and experience, and contact employers to interest them in services of agency.
3	Apply common sense understanding to carry out instructions furnished in written, oral, or diagrammatic form. Deal with problems involving several concrete variables in or from standardized situations.	Make arithmetic calculations involving fractions, decimals, and percentages.	Comprehension and expression of a level to —File, post, and mail such material as forms, checks, receipts, and bills. —Copy data from one record to another, fill in report forms, and type all work from rough draft or corrected copy. —Interview members of household to obtain such information as age, occupation, and number of children, to be used as data for surveys, or economic studies. —Guide people on tours through historical or public buildings, describing such features as size, value, and points of interest.
2	Apply common sense understanding to carry out detailed but uninvolved written or oral instructions. Deal with problems involving a few concrete variables in or from standardized situations.	Use arithmetic to add, subtract, multiply, and divide whole numbers.	
1	Apply common sense understanding to carry out simple one- or two-step instructions. Deal with standardized situations with occasional or no variables in or from these situations encountered on the job.	Perform simple addition and subtraction, reading, and copying of figures, or counting and recording.	Comprehension and expression of a level to —Learn job duties from oral instructions or demonstrations. —Write identifying information, such as name and address of customer, weight, number, or type of product, on tags, or slips. —Request orally, or in writing, such supplies as linen, soap, or work materials.

*Examples of "principles of rational systems" are bookkeeping, internal combustion engines, electric wiring systems, house building, nursing, farm management, and ship sailing.

Source: U.S., Employment Service 1965, vol. 2, p. 652.

This study examines changes in skill requirements over time; therefore, two editions of the DOT are used—the third edition issued in 1965 and the fourth edition issued in 1977.

Information on Workers

In addition to information on the characteristics of jobs, this research requires information on the characteristics of workers, in particular, their educational attainments. This information comes from the U.S. Bureau of the Census. The Census Bureau is responsible for collecting and disseminating information on households and individuals within the United States. Individual information includes personal characteristics (race, sex, age, years of schooling completed) as well as labor market information (current occupation, earnings, hours worked, industry where employed, and so on). These data are collected through a number of different surveys.

Every ten years the Census Bureau conducts a major survey of the population. It issues an extensive series of reports based on these data and makes them available publicly. This study uses the 1/1000 Public Use Sample as a source of information on the status of the working population in the spring of 1960. This sample is actually a random subsample of the 1960 decennial survey. It is described in National Data Use and Access Laboratories (1973).

In addition to conducting the decennial population surveys, the Census Bureau also conducts smaller, monthly surveys of the population in cooperation with the U.S. Bureau of Labor Statistics. These monthly surveys—known as the Current Population Surveys (CPSs)— are used primarily as a source of information on the employment status of the population. In certain months of the year more extensive questionnaires are employed in order to obtain detailed information on the personal characteristics of the working population, including educational attainments and current occupations. The March 1976 CPS (also known as the Annual Demographic File) was used as a source of information on the working population for that year. These data are described in U.S., Bureau of the Census (1977).

A potential problem arises from using different sources of data on the working population. The issue of comparability between these two data sources is addressed in the final section of this chapter.

CONSTRUCTING THE REQUIRED DATA SETS

Since the data used in this study were developed for different purposes and from different sources, a major task of this research involved integrating the data for the purposes of analysis. Fortunately, other researchers using these data have addressed this problem previously (Miller 1971; Lucas 1972; Temme 1975).

The difficulty in merging information on jobs from the DOT and information on people from the census arises, in part, from the different occupational coding systems utilized by the two agencies. The U.S. Employment Service obtains information on every distinct job in the U.S. economy, creating roughly 13,000 individual job categories as well as additional related titles (see U.S., Employment Service 1977, pp. xiii-xli). The U.S. Bureau of the Census uses an occupational classification system based on the socioeconomic status of different jobs (Scoville 1972), a system having little to do with actual job skills. To compound the problem of compatibility, the coding schemes changed between the third and fourth editions of the DOT and between the 1960 and 1976 censuses.

It is possible to go from one classification scheme to the other with the aid of two previous CPSs, October 1966 and March 1971. In these two surveys, respondents' occupations were coded under both systems. Thus job characteristics from the DOT can be assigned to the sample of individuals in the two census surveys. The accuracy of this process is investigated in the last section of this chapter. The following pages discuss the procedures used to construct the two data sets—one for 1960 and one for 1976—used in the empirical chapter that follows.

The 1960 Data Set

Information on job characteristics from the DOT was assigned to individuals' occupations in the 1960 Census Public Use Sample using transformations constructed by Robert Lucas (1972). The October 1966 CPS was coded with both census occupation codes and DOT codes. From this survey Ann Miller (1971) created a matrix that cross-referenced both codes. With this matrix it was possible to determine the probability that a given census occupation code corresponded to a particular DOT occupational code. Lucas used this matrix, together with a data file on the characteristics of jobs from the third edition of the DOT, to assign to every census code the probability of having a particular DOT-defined characteristic (see Lucas 1972, chapter IV). Thus, given a person's census occupation code it is possible to assign to that individual the probability of holding a job with each level of GED.

The final data set used in the empirical analysis was constructed in several steps. First, records of individuals in the civilian labor force (employed and unemployed, 14 years old and over) were extracted from the 1960 1/1000 Public Use Sample. These records contained information on current occupation, education, age, race, and sex. This process yielded a sample of 68,379 individual records. Second, Lucas's data file was used to assign job characteristics to each individual in the sample using the respondent's census occupation code. Lucas had information on 295 out of 297 possible codes, leaving some records without information on job characteristics. Lucas had also subdivided two census categories into ten industry subgroups. Instead of using these subdivided categories, individuals who were coded with one of these two codes were simply assigned the mean values of GED and SVP from the ten subgroups within that particular code. In addition, a number of people in the 1960 census failed to report an occupation, so no DOT information could be assigned to these individuals. After assignment of DOT information to the individual records, the file consisted of the following:

64,935 records with both census and DOT information
   51 records with valid census information but for
      which no corresponding DOT could be found
3,393 records of individuals who failed to report an
      occupation

68,379 total records

Since the DOT information was mandatory for the empirical analysis, those 3,444 cases lacking that information were subsequently dropped from the analysis. This introduced a possible source of error in the resulting estimates, a matter discussed in the last section.

The 1976 Data Set

    A similar set of procedures was employed in constructing the 1976 data set. Individuals in the experienced civilian labor force (employed and unemployed, 14 years old and older), were extracted from the March 1976 CPS, resulting in a total of 58,480 individual records. Again information was extracted on each respondent's occupation, education, age, sex, and race.

    The task of assigning DOT characteristics of jobs to census occupation codes consisted of several steps. A copy of the April 1971 CPS was acquired, which coded respondents with both census occupation codes and DOT codes in the same manner as the October 1966 CPS. This provided a means of cross-classifying census information with information from the third edition of the DOT.

    But a new edition of the DOT was issued in 1977 in which DOT codes were changed and information on job characteristics was up-

dated. In order to get an accurate picture of changes in the characteristics of jobs, particularly in GED levels, it was desirable to compare information from both the third and fourth editions of the DOT.
This comparison required a cross-reference for the two editions of
the DOT. Fortunately, the U.S. Employment Service has created
such a cross-reference and was kind enough to supply a copy of it for
the present research. The cross-reference contained information on
the third and fourth edition DOT codes and titles but not information
on GED and SVP levels. Separate data files, therefore, were used to
obtain information on job characteristics, one for the third edition
and one for the fourth. Information from both the third and fourth
edition master files was assigned to each code in the cross-reference.

This file was then merged with the individual records from the
April 1971 CPS. Not all respondents in the 1971 CPS were assigned
third and fourth edition DOT information. Some respondents did not
report job information and, in some cases, coders from the U.S.
Employment Service were unable to assign a particular DOT code to
a respondent based on the description of the job. The merging of the
1971 CPS file with the DOT cross-reference file resulted in the following:

    51,136 records were successfully assigned third and
              fourth edition DOT information
     8,732 records were not assigned DOT information
      573 records were assigned third edition DOT infor-
              mation but not fourth edition information

    60,441 total records

The 573 records without fourth edition information were due to the
fact that some of the cross-reference DOT codes could not be matched
to information from the fourth edition master file.

This file was then used to assign DOT information to census
codes in a manner similar to that employed by Lucas. The 8,732
records with missing information were not used in the construction
of this file. This omission resulted in potential errors in the estimates of job characteristics, a problem addressed in the last section
of this chapter. From the merged 1971 CPS file each census occupation code was assigned the probability of having each level of GED and
SVP based on both the third and fourth editions of the DOT.[1] In the
case where no fourth edition DOT information was present, the third
edition information was used. The file was then used to assign information to respondents from the 1976 CPS. Again some of the census
occupation codes could not be assigned DOT information because the
1971 CPS file lacked valid information on some census job codes. But
there were only 11 valid census codes that lacked DOT information and

they were occupations in which few people were employed. After merging, the 1976 CPS contained the following:

> 58,444 records with valid third and fourth edition DOT information
> 36 unmatched records
>
> 58,480 total records

Since the number of unmatched records constituted less than 0.1 percent of the total sample, these records were omitted from the analysis.

Although originally both the employed and unemployed were included in the two files, the empirical analyses were ultimately performed on just the employed population. It was felt that this would give a more accurate picture of the jobs that actually exist in the U.S. economy than would estimates that included information on the jobs previously held by the unemployed.

Undoubtedly there are more jobs in the economy than those held by the employed population because at any one point in time there are a number of vacant jobs. But this research deals primarily with distributions and aggregate estimates, so the actual numbers are relatively unimportant. There may be some bias introduced, however, by excluding the unemployed from the analyses. Excluding the unemployed reduced the size of the 1960 data set to 64,945 with an additional 3,023 (4.7 percent) cases deleted because of missing DOT information. The size of the 1976 data set was reduced to 54,194 records with an additional 33 (0.1 percent) cases deleted because of missing DOT information.

THE EMPIRICAL INVESTIGATION

The 1960 and 1976 data sets were used to perform several empirical tasks. The first task involved estimating aggregate distributions of GED levels and educational attainments in both 1960 and 1976. Of primary interest is whether the aggregate distributions of GED levels demonstrate an increase, no change, or a decrease in the overall level of general skill requirements during this period. Figure 1 shows some possible shifts in skill (GED) levels. The distributions shown are only illustrative; there is no reason that they should be symmetrical or conform to a normal distribution. They simply represent two contrasting situations. In the first case, there is an upward shift in the aggregate distribution of skill requirements for jobs in the economy. As the next chapter illustrates, this could result from shifts in employment favoring higher-skilled as opposed to lower-

FIGURE 1

Hypothetical Distribution of GED Levels and Educational Attainments, 1960 and 1976

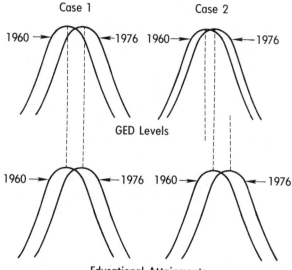

skilled jobs. Such a shift could also result from an upgrading of general skills required to perform the tasks of jobs, possibly due to
technological innovation. The second case illustrates the opposite
situation—a downward shift in the aggregate of skill requirements.
Again such a shift could result from shifts in employment or changes
in the skill requirements of individual jobs. There is no reason that
these two factors should work in the same direction. Shifts in employment may favor higher-skilled jobs, for example, while changes
in requisite job skills may work to lower the aggregate distribution
of skill requirements. This could result in no observed change in
the overall skill requirements of jobs in the economy.

    Comparing the distribution of GED levels with the distribution
of educational attainments will illustrate whether educational attainments (the supply of educational skills brought into the workplace)
are keeping abreast of changes in the skill requirements of jobs (Figure 1, Case 1). Yet there may be a growing divergence between
these two distributions, with the increase in educational attainments
surpassing the growth in demand for educational skills (Case 2).

    In addition to aggregate distributions, a number of disaggre-
gated distributions were produced. One breakdown was performed
for the four major race-sex groups (white males, black males, white

females, and black females). Also, disaggregated distributions were produced for major occupation groups, such as professional, managerial, and clerical occupations. Finally, separate distributions were produced for inexperienced workers.

The second empirical task involved estimating the degree of discrepancy between educational attainments of workers and the skill requirements of their jobs, and analyzing trends in these discrepancies over time. This required a translation of GED levels into equivalent years of schooling. As the next section points out, performing such a conversion is a formidable problem. But once such an equivalency is established, it is possible to calculate mean years of overeducation for each respondent in the sample as follows:

$$\text{Overeducation (in years)} = \text{Years of schooling completed} - \text{GED levels (in years)}$$

In addition to examining changes in the overall levels of overeducation between the two years, the relationship between years of overeducation and years of schooling was estimated with the equation:[2]

$$\text{Overed} = \alpha + \sum_{i=1}^{n} \beta_i X_i + \epsilon$$

where

$$\text{Overed} = \text{years of overeducation}$$
$$X_i = \text{dummy variables representing years of schooling completed}$$

The coefficients of this equation were estimated using ordinary least squares regression. This expression estimates the discrepancy between the educational attainments of workers and the educational requirements of their jobs (overeducation) by schooling level. It indicates whether overeducation affects only workers with high levels of schooling or whether the condition plagues the entire working population. Estimating the coefficients with both the 1960 and 1976 data illustrates trends in this relationship between the two years.

It is possible that overeducation primarily affects new entrants into the labor force rather than both experienced and inexperienced workers. Some observers have argued, for example, that recent college graduates are failing to find jobs commensurate with their level of training. Furthermore, if overeducation is primarily a recent phenomenon, new entrants in 1960 may not have experienced it to the same degree as new entrants in 1976.

The third task of this research involved testing these proposi-
The incidence of overeducation was calculated for new entrants—work-

ers with only a few years of work experience. The data lacked information on years of experience, so the variable was estimated as follows:

Years of experience = Age - Years of schooling completed - 6

Those with estimated experience levels between zero and five years were designated <u>new entrants</u>. Obviously this approach is subject to error. It assigns years of experience based on a normal progression through school. For example, individuals currently working at age 18 with 12 years of school completed are assumed to have no years of work experience. Yet they may have graduated at age 17 and have 1 year of work experience. This procedure also fails to distinguish between those who are working or have worked full-time and part-time. A year of part-time work experience may not be the same as a year of full-time experience. In spite of these shortcomings, this approach is the best available one for assigning years of experience within the limitations of the available data.[3]

The estimates produced from these tasks are used to answer the following questions:

1. How have the general skill requirements of jobs in the U.S. economy changed between 1960 and 1976?
2. How have the educational attainments of the work force changed during this same period?
3. Has there been a growing discrepancy between these two and, if so, in what direction?
4. How has the relationship between years of overeducation and education itself changed over this period, both on the aggregate level and for young, inexperienced workers?

The empirical results and the answers to these questions appear in the next chapter. The remainder of this chapter deals with the issue of inaccuracies in the empirical estimates.

SOURCES OF BIAS AND ERROR
IN THE PROPOSED ESTIMATES

As the preceding discussion pointed out, there are several possible sources of bias and error in the empirical part of this study. In general, it is difficult to assess the degree to which the results may be biased. A small percentage of the data is known to be inaccurate, mostly due to missing information. This should introduce little error. What is more important, however, is whether or not the errors are random. There is no evidence to indicate that the errors should not be random. For example, if there were inaccuracies in determining a respondent's actual occupation from the census questionnaire the estimates of job skill requirements may be inaccurate. Yet there is no reason to suspect that such inaccuracies systematically overstate (or understate) actual skill requirements. Moreover, since the procedures used to estimate skill requirements were the same for the 1960 data set as for the 1976 data set, any resulting bias should be similar. Comparisons between the two years should, therefore, accurately reflect actual changes. Instances where the biases in the two data sets may be dissimilar are pointed out below.

Assigning GED Information to Census Data

One potential source of error arises from the attempt to accurately assign DOT information on job characteristics to census occupation codes. As pointed out in the third section, a number of respondents from the 1971 CPS either failed to report an occupation or provided insufficient information with which to assign a DOT code. This problem arises from the nature of the CPS questionnaire, which contained only one question about the respondent's job: "What kind of work was . . . doing?" during the week before the survey. With such nondetailed information, the ability of coders to accurately assign each respondent to one of over 13,000 particular codes must be questioned. In spite of this potential source of inaccuracy, CPS data allow one to observe the distribution of DOT-coded jobs within each census job category. This increases the accuracy of the estimates of skill requirements for census job categories by accounting for the composite of DOT-coded jobs and their estimated skill requirements within each census job category. Without these distributions, an unweighted composite estimate of skill requirements would have to be used to estimate the skill requirements of census job categories. [4]

The accuracy with which DOT codes can be assigned to census occupation codes is only one potential source of error in the estimates of job characteristics. In the 1971 CPS the number of individuals who were not assigned DOT information is known. This information is unavailable for the 1966 CPS data that Lucas used to assign DOT information to census job categories. It is likely that there was a similar number of unassigned individuals, since a similar CPS questionnaire was used.

In addition, there may be a different distribution of DOT jobs held by persons of different race or sex even within a particular census category. This would most likely arise in those census categories that cover a heterogeneous group of occupations (such as, managers and administrators, not elsewhere classified). Producing one distribution of job requirements for each census code and assigning it to all individuals with that code will overstate the characteristics

of jobs held by blacks to the degree that blacks hold worse jobs or
lower-skilled jobs than whites, even within the same census job category. This bias may be weaker for women since the majority are employed in jobs predominantly held by women (Lucas 1972, p. 125).[5]
Finally, since only cases with both DOT and census codes were used
to estimate these distributions, there is no way of knowing to what extent those excluded cases resulted in errors in these estimates.

It is difficult to evaluate the seriousness of these errors and the
degree to which they influence the empirical results. Because the
procedures and data used in the construction of the 1960 and 1976 data
sets were similar, any errors should at least influence results from
the two years similarly. In addition, since many of the estimated
distributions were on an aggregate level, the inaccuracy may be quite
small, with errors in each direction balancing out.

Differences between Censuses and the DOT

Another source of bias stems from differences between the various data sets. First, there is the question of the accuracy of the occupational information in the two censuses and their comparability.
The questionnaire used to obtain information on occupations was
changed between the two years. In 1960 the survey used a question
similar to the one in the April 1971 CPS that asked what work the respondent was doing the week prior to the survey (U.S., Bureau of the
Census 1972, p. 152). An additional question was added to the CPS
questionnaire beginning in the fall of 1971 that asked the principal activities performed by the respondents in their jobs (U.S., Bureau of
the Census and U.S., Bureau of Labor Statistics 1976). Thus occupational information from the 1976 CPS is undoubtedly more accurate
than occupational information from the 1960 census.[6] Also, part of
the sample in 1960 (4.7 percent) failed to report an occupation, adding
further inaccuracy to the 1960 occupational information.

An additional source of bias in the estimates arises from making
comparisons between 1960 and 1976 using the third and fourth editions
of the DOT. The information on job characteristics from the third
edition of the DOT was released in 1965 and was probably collected in
1963 and 1964. Assigning GED levels to census occupation codes in
1960 based on that edition of the DOT may overstate the actual skill
requirements of jobs in that year to the degree that they were lower
than in 1963 and 1964. This problem is less acute in the 1976 data
file since the fourth edition DOT information on job characteristics
was collected close to the time of the March 1976 CPS. The bias in
the 1960 data also means that comparisons or changes in skill requirements between 1960 and 1976 may be understated. Consequently,

changes in the degree of overeducation between the two years may be overstated. Of course, if actual skill requirements declined between 1960 and the time of the third edition of the DOT, then the degree of overeducation between 1960 and 1976 may be understated.

Another problem arises from using the cross-reference file to translate third edition DOT codes in the 1971 CPS into equivalent fourth edition codes. Between the third and fourth editions of the DOT, some occupation codes were added and some were deleted. In the case of added codes, this means that some occupations in the 1971 CPS sample may have been coded with a particular third edition DOT code when another fourth edition code would have represented that occupation more accurately. But unless the new codes created in the fourth edition of the DOT are, on average, associated with higher skill levels than third edition codes (recent evidence suggests they are not—see Spenner 1979, p. 971), estimated skill levels for census occupation codes should be reasonably accurate. The problem with deleted codes was minor. In the 1971 CPS sample, fewer than .10 percent of the cases with third edition codes were not matched to fourth edition codes. In these instances, third edition information was used.

Finally, it was assumed that the estimates of job characteristics, particularly GED levels, in the fourth edition of the DOT were independent of estimates in the third edition. This may not be the case, however. In some instances estimates of GED levels in the fourth edition may have come from third edition estimates, and not from new evaluations of job content (Miller et al. forthcoming). Thus the skill content of specific jobs as well as changes in skill levels of jobs between successive editions of the DOT may be understated.

Independence of GED Estimates and
Worker Characteristics

Another source of error in the estimates of overeducation may come from the estimates of skill requirements in the DOT. It is fundamental to this study that the skill requirements of jobs are determined independently from the educational attainments of workers occupying those jobs. As pointed out previously, there is a distinct difference between the functional or performance requirements of jobs and the hiring requirements of jobs dictated by employers. Employers, in the face of a loose labor market where there is an oversupply of highly educated workers, may have a tendency to raise the educational requirements of jobs even though such increased requirements have little to do with changes in the content of the work performed. The increase in the number of college graduates entering the labor force during the last 15 years may have prompted such action. Changes in the skill requirements between the two latest editions of the DOT should reflect changes in skill requirements due to actual increases in the tasks of jobs and not changes in employers' tastes for certain worker traits. It is worthwhile to review briefly the procedures that the U.S. Employment Service uses to estimate the skill requirements of jobs in the economy.

The procedures are outlined in a U.S., Department of Labor (1972) publication, Handbook for Analyzing Jobs. Job analysts collect information about the actual work performed on the job as well as required worker traits (including training time). Most information is collected by observation and interview. "This method involves analyzing jobs by observing workers performing their jobs and interviewing workers, supervisors, and others who have information pertinent to the job" (p. 12). If this method is impossible to use, the analyst may obtain information from job descriptions furnished by establishments and associations as well as from interviews conducted away from the work setting (p. 14). The procedures for evaluating and recording training time requirements are based on two questions (p. 229):

What level of general educational development is required for a worker to acquire the background knowledge and to follow the instructions in the specific job/worker situations?

How long in terms of specific vocational preparation does it take for a worker of specified general educational development to become a fully qualified worker, in contrast to a trainee, in this job?

In addition, separate information is collected on the following requirements for each job: general education, vocational preparation, and experience. In the latter case, the employer can express a preference, although the analyst may disagree based on the ratings given for GED and SVP (p. 25). But from the instructions in the manual, worker traits (including GED and SVP) should always be compared with the detailed description of the tasks in order "to insure that each reflects the other and that no essential information is omitted" (p. 28).

According to these procedures, information on functional requirements of jobs is collected separately from employer requirements. This should ensure the independence of requisite worker traits and the supply of educational skills in the market. But because a number of techniques are employed by job analysts to obtain information on jobs, there is no guarantee that recorded GED and SVP levels are completely independent from employer preferences.

Equating Skill Requirements and Years of Schooling

Finally, a potential source of inaccuracy in constructing the proposed estimates comes from translating skill requirements into equivalent years of schooling. The difficulty exists because the two measures were not designed to be equivalent. The U.S. Employment Service collects specific information on the desired worker traits for jobs, including skill requirements, while years of schooling only serve as an approximate estimate of acquired skills. One year of schooling could mean different levels of skill development depending on the type of courses studied, the ability of the particular student, and the quality of the institution attended.

A translation is further complicated by the relationship between GED and SVP levels themselves. In general, GED is more nearly equivalent to the training acquired in school, while SVP measures job-specific skills acquired from school, on-the-job training, and experience. But there is some overlap between the two. A year of school could develop general skills related to GED, or it could develop job-specific skills related to SVP. A footnote in the Handbook for Analyzing Jobs states (p. 209):

> In evaluating training time information on jobs, observe the following standards: (1) Regard 30 hours of high school shop or commercial training as equivalent to about 15 hours of on-the-job training; (2) regard the average 4-year college curriculum (except for liberal arts) as equivalent to about 2 years of specific vocational preparation; (3) regard each year of graduate schooling as a year of specific vocational preparation.

Thus a four-year undergraduate degree could relate exclusively to GED preparation (in the case of liberal arts majors) or relate to both GED preparation and SVP (for other majors). This makes equating GED and years of schooling difficult. In addition, the census data used in this study only includes information on the number of years of schooling completed, not the subjects studied in school, the amount and type of other vocational training, or relevant experience. So any translation of GED levels into equivalent years of schooling can only be approximate.

Nonetheless, translations have been made by other researchers (Eckaus 1964; Scoville 1966; Berg 1970; Kolstad 1976). One conversion was first proposed by Eckaus (1964). The U.S. Employment Service, in a manual prepared for field offices to assist job applicants in their search for suitable employment, has suggested another conversion (U.S., Department of Labor 1971). These two conversions

TABLE 4

GED Levels and Equivalent Years of Schooling

GED Level	Equivalent Years of Schooling	
	Conversion I	Conversion II
1	0- 4	0- 3
2	5- 7	4- 6
3	8-10	7- 8
4	11-12	9-12
5	13-16	13-14
6	17-18	15-16

Sources: Eckaus (1964); U.S., Department of Labor (1971).

are illustrated in Table 4. The equivalencies proposed by Eckaus allocate higher levels of schooling to each GED level than those of the Department of Labor. There is no way to determine which conversion is more accurate, so both were employed in the aggregate analyses in order to see how they affected the results.[7] Only further empirical research can determine an accurate translation of GED levels into years of schooling.

In assigning yearly equivalents of GED levels for equation 2 above, the highest schooling level associated with each GED level was used. For example, GED level 6 was equated with 18 years of schooling under conversion I and 16 years of schooling under conversion II.

SUMMARY

The methodology employed in the empirical part of this study is straightforward, yet it was difficult to implement. Two data sets, one for 1960 and one for 1976, were constructed from census records of individuals in the employed labor force. These records contained information on the educational attainment and current occupation of each individual. The primary methodological task involved estimating the educational requirements of jobs from DOT information. Each step used to accomplish this task introduced a potential source of error in the empirical estimates. Based on a review of these sources, however, it does not appear that these errors systematically biased the empirical estimates.

NOTES

1. The fourth edition GED scale was composed of three components, as illustrated in Table 3. The third edition GED scale was reduced to a one-dimensional scale representing the highest of the three component scores. In order to ensure comparability between the two editions, the highest of the component scores was also used as a single GED score in the fourth edition estimates.

2. This is essentially the same equation used by Lucas (1972, p. 185).

3. Welch and Gould (1976) have developed a means of estimating years of experience that accounts for differences in progression through school.

4. Other attempts have been made to cross-classify census and DOT occupation codes that were based primarily on taking detailed DOT job descriptions and their corresponding codes first and then assigning them to particular census codes, instead of the other way around, as was the case for the 1966 and 1971 CPS data (see U.S., Bureau of Labor Statistics 1975; State of California 1976). The problem with these methods is that there is no way of knowing the distribution of DOT jobs within each census category.

5. This assumption is questionable, however. Sexton (1977, pp. 39-40) reviews evidence suggesting that the skill requirements of some predominantly female occupations are underrated in the DOT. This raises a more fundamental question about the accuracy of the skill estimates themselves, an issue that warrants further investigation.

6. A recent census publication examines the accuracy of occupational information received in the CPS questionnaire. (See U.S., Bureau of the Census 1978).

7. Berg (1970, chap. 3) used a number of possible conversions in his analyses.

4

EMPIRICAL RESULTS

INTRODUCTION

The previous chapter raised a number of questions about the incidence of overeducation. In this chapter the empirical results are used to formulate answers to these questions. The investigation focuses primarily on the years 1960 and 1976 and consists of three parts. The first part deals with the demand for general skills in the economy: specifically, how the skill requirements of jobs in the U. S. economy changed during this period. It is often assumed implicitly that the skill requirements of jobs are rising. There is a popular faith that as society "advances" the evolving technology will release workers from boring, repetitious, and physical tasks and will substitute more challenging mental tasks requiring more complex and varied skills.

Others have challenged this belief (Mills 1951; Braverman 1974). Critics argue that the logic of capitalist development necessarily results in the fragmentation of work tasks, resulting in an overall reduction in the skill requirements of jobs in the economy. Their assessment is that labor is being degraded rather than being elevated. These viewpoints are so contradictory that the issue of whether skill requirements are rising or falling becomes important in understanding the evolution of work in contemporary society. This issue is addressed in the first section by examining changes in the aggregate distributions of general skills in the U. S. economy between 1960 and 1976 as reflected in levels of General Educational Development (GED).

The second part of this investigation focuses on the supply of skills brought into the labor market. Educational attainments serve as a proxy for general skills. Although it is well known that the educational attainments of the population have been rising throughout this period, it is important to document the extent of this change because it directly affects the degree of overeducation observed in the labor market.

The third part of the empirical analysis involves the measurement of overeducation itself. Overeducation is measured by contrasting the educational attainments of the working population with the general skill requirements of their jobs.[1] The first estimates for the entire working population compare the aggregate distributions of educational attainments and job skill requirements as reflected in GED levels. These distributions are then disaggregated by race and sex in order to compare intergroup differences and assess how they have changed over time. Next, the number of years of overeducation is estimated by schooling level based on equation 2 from the previous chapter. Finally, the investigation focuses on the changing situation for the most recent entrants into the labor market, the inexperienced working population. It is within this group that the most profound changes in the incidence of overeducation may be found. Recent college graduates, for example, are said to be experiencing the greatest difficulty in finding jobs commensurate with their level of training.

After focusing on the period between 1960 and 1976, the last section examines how this situation might change by projecting the incidence of overeducation to 1985. The final section of the chapter will summarize the important findings.

CHANGES IN SKILL REQUIREMENTS, 1960-76

Changes in the aggregate distribution of job skills in the economy result from two independent actions: shifts in the distribution of jobs in the economy and changes in the skill requirements of individual jobs. In the first instance, changes in the distribution of employment among jobs result in changes in the observed distribution of job skills. Jobs vary with respect to the amount or complexity of skills required to perform their respective tasks. For example, the job of physician probably requires more skill than the job of common laborer. But other differences are less clear, such as between a teacher and a laboratory technician or between a secretary and a cook. The point is simply that different jobs require different amounts of skill and that shifts in employment between jobs will undoubtedly affect the overall distribution of job skills observed in the economy.

Changes in the requisite skills of particular jobs will also influence the aggregate distribution of skills in the economy. Over time the tasks of some jobs vary as a result of changes in the organization of work. It is often assumed that technology, more than any other factor, is responsible for changing the tasks of jobs and therefore their requisite job skills. For example, many office jobs now involve the use of computers and electronic word-processing equipment, which are said to require more skills (Shepard 1971). Changes in technology and the organization of work will therefore lead to changes in the requisite skills of jobs in the economy, which will affect the aggregate distribution of observed job skills.

These two factors act independently of each other; there is no reason why they should produce shifts in the same direction. Shifts in employment between jobs and changes in the skill requirements of individual jobs could both act to increase the overall distribution of job skills, or act to decrease the distribution of job skills, or tend to move the distribution in opposite directions. In the latter case, the observed distribution of skill requirements could remain unchanged.

In the following discussion, the effects of shifts in employment and changes in the skill requirements of individual jobs are examined separately. First, consider shifts in employment. Table 5 shows the distribution of employment among major occupation groups in 1960 and 1976. The occupation groups are defined according to the census classification scheme, since it is the most widely used and well-known system for examining employment patterns. The figures in Table 5 show that between 1960 and 1976 the percentage of workers employed in all white-collar occupations (except sales workers) and in service occupations (except private household workers) increased, while the percentage of workers employed in blue-collar and farming occupations decreased in this period. The growth in white-collar employment itself is often heralded as an indication of the increasing employment opportunities in the more rewarding and demanding portion of the job hierarchy. But the terms white-collar and blue-collar actually reveal little about job content or requisite job skills. As Aronowitz (1973, p. 292) states,

> "White-collar" is a label that presupposes an essential
> difference between the structure of labor in the factory
> and in the office. It is a category of social ideology rather
> than of social science and has evoked the image of a system
> of social stratification that regards office work as a higher-
> status occupation than factory work, administration as more
> prestigious than manual labor, or, indeed, any occupation
> related directly to the production of goods. The bare fact
> is that "white-collar" is less a description of an actual
> group of workers than a conceptual tool for a specific per-
> spective on social class.

In reality some blue-collar jobs may require far more skills than many white-collar jobs. Thus, changes in the distribution of employment favoring white-collar occupations will not necessarily increase the overall distribution of skill requirements in the economy.

TABLE 5

Distribution of Employment by Occupation Group
for the Employed Population, 1960 and 1976

	1960	1976
White-collar workers	43.1	50.1
Professional and technical workers	11.9	15.2
Managers and administrators	8.6	10.6
Sales workers	7.6	6.5
Clerical workers	15.0	17.8
Blue-collar workers	38.5	32.4
Craft and kindred workers	14.1	12.6
Operatives	19.3	15.2
Nonfarm laborers	5.1	4.6
Service workers	11.6	14.4
Private household workers	2.8	1.8
Other service workers	8.8	12.6
Farm workers	6.7	3.2
Farmers	4.2	1.7
Farm laborers	2.5	1.5
Total	100.0	100.0

Note: Percentage distributions may not add to 100.0 because
of rounding.

The effects of shifts in employment on the aggregate distribution
of skills in the economy are illustrated in Table 6, columns 1 and 2.[2]
Column 1 shows the aggregate distribution of skill requirements in
1960 based on the third edition of the Dictionary of Occupational Titles
(DOT); column 2 shows the distribution of skill requirements in 1976
based on the third edition of the DOT. Changes in these distributions
are due to changes in the distribution of employment between the two
years, not to changes in the skill requirements of individual jobs.
The results show an increase in the two highest skill levels (GED levels 5 and 6), corresponding to skills normally acquired in college,
and a decrease in the percentage of workers having jobs in the lowest
four levels (high school or less). These changes confirm the popular
notion that shifts in employment have raised the overall skill requirements of jobs in the economy.

Next consider the effect of changes in the skill requirements of
individual jobs. Column 3 in Table 6 shows the distribution of skill
requirements in 1976 based on the fourth edition of the DOT. Differ-

TABLE 6

Distribution of GED Levels of Jobs for the Employed Population,
1960 and 1976

GED Level	1 1960 DOT3[a]	2 1976 DOT3[b]	3 1976 DOT4[c]
1	2.2	1.9	1.6
2	13.5	13.0	13.2
3	35.1	32.2	29.8
4	33.6	33.0	35.4
5	11.0	14.2	16.1
6	4.3	5.4	3.6

[a]Distribution of GED levels in 1960 based on the third edition of
the DOT.
[b]Distribution of GED levels in 1976 based on the third edition of
the DOT.
[c]Distribution of GED levels in 1976 based on the fourth edition
of the DOT.

Note: Percentage distributions may not add to 100.0 because
of rounding.

ences between columns 2 and 3 provide an estimate of changes in skill
requirements between 1960 and 1976 owing solely to revisions in the
estimates of skill requirements between the third and fourth editions
of the DOT. The results are unexpected: revisions in the DOT actually reduced the percentage of highly skilled jobs (GED level 6),
although the percentage of jobs requiring middle-level skills (GED
levels 3 to 5) did increase in this period.

The net result of these changes was to increase the percentage
of jobs in the upper-middle range of skills (GED levels 4 and 5).
But because of revisions in the DOT estimates of skill requirements,
the percentage of jobs at the highest skill level (GED level 6) actually
declined, in spite of shifts in employment favoring more skilled jobs.
There were also decreases in the percentage of low-skilled jobs (GED
levels 1 to 3).

The observed decrease in the percentage of jobs corresponding
to GED level 6 compares favorably with the findings of Berg (1970).
Using a different methodology, he constructed distributions of GED
levels for the labor force for 1950 and 1960, with the 1950 data based
on the second edition of the DOT and the 1960 data based on the third

edition of the DOT. Controlling for changes in employment between the two years, he observed a decrease in the skill requirements of jobs at each end of the distribution owing to revisions in the DOT (pp. 48-49).

To summarize, the overall effects of shifts in the composition of employment in the economy and changes in the skill requirements of individual jobs between 1960 and 1976 resulted in the movement of the aggregate distribution of skills toward the middle and upper-middle and away from the ends of the range. In other words, the distribution of job skills within the U.S. economy appeared to narrow during this period. The estimates probably understate the degree of actual change that took place since the third edition estimates of GED levels were made circa 1963 and 1964. The most startling finding was the decrease in the percentage of jobs requiring the highest level of skills, a decrease owing solely to revisions in the estimates of skill requirements by the U.S. Employment Service as contained in the fourth edition of the DOT.

CHANGES IN EDUCATIONAL
ATTAINMENTS, 1960-76

Having examined the demand for skills within the labor market between 1960 and 1976, this section focuses on the supply of those skills in the labor market during the same period. Educational attainments will serve as an index of job skills to the market, although the previous chapter discussed some of the strengths and weaknesses of education as a skill indicator.

The educational system experienced phenomenal growth during the period between 1960 and 1976, especially at the postsecondary level. Enrollment in higher education increased greatly during this period because of two concurrent developments. First, the 18-to-24-year-old population, from which the majority of the participants in higher education have traditionally been drawn, almost doubled during this period (Grant and Lind 1979, p. 91). Second, the percentage of the population participating in higher education also increased during this same period. In fact, the largest increases in participation rates were registered in the nontraditional age groups (individuals 25 years old and over) who accounted for almost one-third of all college students by 1974 (Golladay 1976, p. 226). These two developments led to a threefold increase in total enrollment between 1960 and 1976 (Grant and Lind 1979, p. 91), resulting in a spectacular growth in the number of degrees awarded, especially at the bachelor's level (see Figure 2).

Changes in the educational attainments of the work force reflect the growth in the educational system during this period. Table 7 shows

FIGURE 2

Bachelor's and Master's Degrees Earned, 1940–74

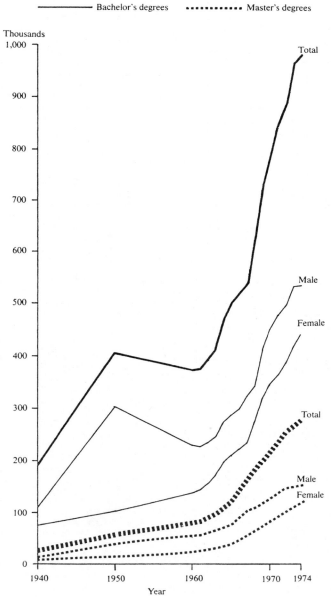

Source: Golladay 1976, p. 38.

73

TABLE 7

Distribution of Educational Attainments
for the Employed Population, 1960 and 1976

Years of Schooling Completed	1960	1976
0-8	30.3	11.2
9-11	21.9	16.6
12	27.7	39.0
13-15	10.5	15.9
16	5.6	9.9
17	1.7	2.2
18 and over	2.3	4.6
Total	100.0	100.0

Note: Percentage distributions may not add to 100.0 because of rounding.

the distribution of educational attainments for the working population in 1960 and 1976. These figures reveal an upward shift in the years of schooling completed by persons employed in the labor force. There were significant reductions in the percentage of the working population with less than 12 years of schooling during this period and corresponding increases in the percentage of persons with 12 or more years of schooling. By 1976 nearly one-third (32.6 percent) of the working population had completed at least one year of college while close to one-fifth (16.7 percent) had completed at least four years of college.

CHANGES IN THE INCIDENCE OF
OVEREDUCATION, 1960-76

In the preceding sections the distributions of educational attainments in the working population and the skill requirements of their jobs were examined independently. This section estimates discrepancies between these two distributions in order to measure the incidence of overeducation.

A number of estimates are constructed based on the two population groups. The first group of estimates is based on the entire working population. First, an analysis is done of the incidence of overeducation in 1960 and 1976 using aggregate distributions of educational attainments and skill requirements. Then an examination is made of

similar distributions disaggregated by race and sex in order to see
whether the incidence of overeducation varies among these groups.
Finally, an estimate is presented of the years of overeducation by
schooling level based on equation 2 from the previous chapter. These
same procedures are then applied to the second group, the inexperienced working population. Comparisons between the two groups will
help determine whether new labor market entrants are experiencing
a higher incidence of overeducation than the working population as a
whole.

The Incidence of Overeducation
in the Working Population

One way to measure overeducation is simply to contrast the distribution of educational attainments with the distribution of skill requirements for the working population. Table 8 shows the distribution of skill requirements, as indexed by GED levels, contrasted with
the distribution of equivalent levels of educational attainments for the
years 1960 and 1976. Recall from the previous chapter that there is
no clearly acceptable criterion for equating years of schooling to GED
levels, so two possible conversions are shown (see Table 4). Conversion I is based on an equivalency first proposed by Eckaus (1964) and
probably represents a conservative estimate. The other conversion
was taken from a Department of Labor publication and probably represents a more liberal equivalency (U.S., Department of Labor 1971).
   The distribution shown in Table 8 is illustrated graphically in
Figure 3. A perfect correspondence between the two distributions
(skill requirements and equivalent years of schooling) would result
in identical distributions. This is not the case, however. There was
little change in the distribution of skill requirements (as reflected in
GED levels) between 1960 and 1976—only a slight shift occurred in the
middle of the distribution, with decreases at the extreme ends. The
distribution of educational attainments, on the other hand, shifted
dramatically during this period. Based on conversion I, there was
not much discrepancy between the distributions of educational attainments and GED levels in 1960; there was only some mismatch in the
middle of the distributions, indicating some degree of overeducation.
But by 1976 the distribution of education had shifted significantly to
higher levels. In particular, less than one-quarter of the working
population had educational attainments corresponding to the bottom
three GED levels, while nearly half (44.6 percent) held jobs with
skill requirements at those levels. As older workers with less than
a high school education leave the labor force and as secondary schooling has become nearly universal, the population is reaching a point

TABLE 8

Distribution of GED Levels and Educational Attainments
for the Employed Population, 1960 and 1976

| Level | GED | Educational Attainments | |
		I	II
1960			
1	2.2	4.8	3.1
2	13.5	11.0	7.2
3	35.1	29.6	19.9
4	33.6	34.4	49.6
5	11.0	16.2	8.4
6	4.3	4.0	11.7
1976			
1	1.6	1.8	1.2
2	13.2	4.1	2.8
3	29.8	16.8	7.9
4	35.4	44.7	55.5
5	16.1	25.8	13.2
6	3.6	6.8	19.4

Note: Educational attainments are grouped into categories corresponding to equivalencies shown in Table 4. Percentage distributions may not add to 100.0 because of rounding.

where almost everyone has completed 11 or 12 years of schooling.
Yet the skill requirements of jobs are failing to move upward at the
same rate.

Comparisons based on conversion II paint an even gloomier picture. They show that, even in 1960, there was a fair degree of incongruence between educational attainments and skill requirements,
especially in the middle ranges of the distribution (GED levels 3 and
4). By 1976, the discrepancies were even more pronounced, particularly at the higher levels. Conversion II equates more years of
schooling to GED level 6 (14 years or more) than does conversion I
(17 years or more) and less to GED level 5. Consequently, comparisons based on conversion II show greater disparities between the percentage of the population with educational qualifications equivalent to
GED level 6 and the percentage of jobs held by the working population
with requisite skills at that level. Conversely, based on conversion

FIGURE 3

Distribution of GED Levels and Educational Attainments
for the Employed Population, 1960 and 1976

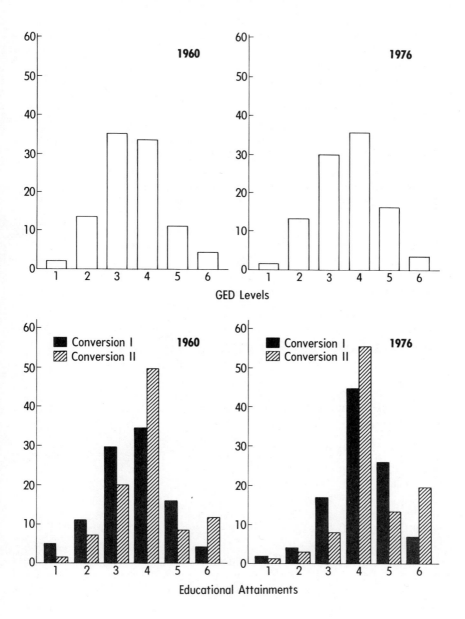

GED Levels

Educational Attainments

II, only a small percentage (11.9 percent) of employed persons had educational attainments corresponding to the lowest three levels of skill requirements, while almost half (44.6 percent) of the jobs they held corresponded to those levels. On the other hand, a large majority (88.1 percent) of this group possessed educational attainments corresponding to the upper three levels, while less than one-half (44.1 percent) of their jobs fell into those categories. Using either conversion, by 1976 one-third of the employed population had at least some college (13 or more years of schooling), while only one-fifth of the jobs in the economy required that level of schooling (GED levels 5 and 6). Thus, about 40 percent of all college-educated workers in 1976 were overeducated for their jobs.

As was pointed out in Chapter 1, other researchers have observed disparities between the educational attainments of the labor force and the skill requirements of their jobs based on GED levels. In particular, Berg, Freedman, and Freeman (1978, chap. 6) report results similar to those presented here—little change in the distributions of skill requirements of jobs between 1960 and 1970 in contrast to large increases in the educational attainments of workers.[3]

How does the incidence of overeducation vary by race and sex? Table 9 shows the distributions of GED levels and equivalent years of schooling by race and sex for 1960 and 1976. Only equivalent years of schooling based on conversion I are shown, which may present a conservative estimate of the degree of overeducation. But since the primary interest is in making comparisons among race and sex groups, the differences between the conversion systems are less important here.

Disregarding changes between 1960 and 1976 for the moment, there are some important differences in the distributions among the four groups. According to the distributions of GED levels, whites were better represented in the higher-skilled jobs (GED levels 5 and 6) than blacks, especially black males, in both years. Conversely, blacks were concentrated more heavily in lower-skilled jobs than whites. The patterns of educational attainment are much the same; whites had higher educational attainments than blacks, who were better represented in the lower levels.

The changes in these distributions between 1960 and 1976 were similar to those observed on the aggregate level: there were slight changes in the distribution of GED levels and upward shifts in the distribution of education for all groups. But there were also changes particular to one group or another. Although blacks continued to hold a smaller percentage of higher-skilled jobs than whites in 1976, they did make some improvements in their relative standing between 1960 and 1976. For example, the percentage of blacks holding jobs at GED level 5 doubled during this period compared with roughly a 50

TABLE 9

Distribution of GED Levels and Educational Attainments for the
Employed Population by Race and Sex, 1960 and 1976

| | Males | | | | Females | | | |
| | White | | Black | | White | | Black | |
Level	1960	1976	1960	1976	1960	1976	1960	1976
GED levels								
1	2.0	1.7	5.9	4.7	7.0	1.1	11.1	3.0
2	12.8	13.6	31.2	23.8	10.6	10.8	21.3	17.6
3	31.3	24.6	38.9	36.4	39.7	35.2	53.8	43.1
4	36.4	38.4	17.9	25.5	33.2	34.1	13.4	20.4
5	11.0	16.3	3.2	7.5	12.8	16.9	7.6	14.8
6	5.8	5.2	1.5	2.0	1.9	1.8	0.8	1.0
Educational attainments								
1 (0–4)	4.2	1.7	20.5	6.9	1.9	1.0	11.7	3.0
2 (5–7)	11.1	4.3	23.5	10.9	7.0	2.8	21.3	6.4
3 (8–10)	31.1	17.2	28.7	22.7	27.0	15.5	28.2	18.9
4 (11–12)	32.4	41.3	19.4	40.6	42.8	50.3	26.2	47.9
5 (13–16)	16.5	27.0	6.5	16.1	18.0	25.4	11.0	20.5
6 (17–18)	4.7	8.5	1.4	2.7	3.2	5.0	1.6	3.2

Note: Equivalent years of schooling (numbers in parentheses)
are based on conversion I, Table 4. Percentage distributions may
not add to 100.0 because of rounding.

percent increase for whites. Also, there were small gains made at
the highest level (GED level 6). The percentage of white and black
women employed in jobs requiring the least skills (GED level 1) declined appreciably in this same period. There were similar gains in
educational attainments: dramatic decreases in the percentage of
lower educated blacks (levels 1 and 2) and corresponding gains in the
upper levels (levels 3–5). Increases in the highest level of educational attainments were similar for all groups.

What do these distributions indicate about the incidence of overeducation among these four groups? At the highest level (6), women
were the most overeducated; they exhibited greater relative discrepancies between the percentage of the jobs they held at that level and
their educational attainments compared with men. But among the top

two levels (5 and 6), black males were the most overeducated. Almost one-fifth (18.8 percent) of all black males had completed some college by 1976, yet only one-tenth (9.5 percent) held jobs requiring that corresponding level of skill. In contrast, almost one-quarter (23.7 percent) of black females had educational attainments corresponding to those levels, while 15.8 percent were employed in jobs at those levels.

By and large, it appears that the incidence of overeducation exists for all groups in the labor market. Whites, on the average, possess higher levels of educational attainment but are better represented in the higher-skilled occupations than are blacks.

In order to get an idea of how the incidence of overeducation varies by level of schooling, mean years of overeducation were regressed on years of schooling according to equation 2 presented in the previous chapter. Separate regressions were run for white males, black males, white females, and black females for 1960 and 1976. These analyses indicate whether individuals with more years of schooling are generally more overeducated for their jobs than are persons with less schooling. They also illustrate how this relationship varies among persons of different race and sex.

Table 10 shows the regression results for the entire working population. Years of schooling are represented by dummy variables. The coefficients of these variables, therefore, estimate years of overeducation by schooling level relative to the omitted dummy variable—in this case, 12 years of schooling. The constant term represents an estimate of years of overeducation for persons with 12 years of schooling. Estimated years of overeducation by schooling level are graphically illustrated in Figure 4.

These estimates point out how the incidence of overeducation varies by schooling level between whites and blacks, males and females. In general, blacks are more overeducated for the jobs that they hold than are whites, except at the highest schooling levels. Women and men show roughly the same degree of overeducation by schooling levels. All groups display a similar relationship between years of schooling and years of overeducation—the least-educated workers are the least overeducated while the most-educated workers are the most overeducated. In fact, those in the lowest education groups (less than 12 years of schooling) were actually undereducated for their jobs. They held jobs requiring more educational skills than they appear to possess. Lucas (1972, pp. 184-89) observed a similar relationship for workers in 1966. This finding raises the question of how those workers can perform satisfactorily in their jobs if the specified relationship between GED levels and education is accurate (see the discussion by Scoville 1966).

There were some interesting changes that took place between 1960 and 1976 for males. White males in all schooling categories

TABLE 10

Estimated Years of Overeducation by Schooling Level for the Employed Population
by Race and Sex, 1960 and 1976

	Males				Females			
	White		Black		White		Black	
	1960	1976	1960	1976	1960	1976	1960	1976
Years of schooling								
0–8	-4.27[a]	-4.21[a]	-6.23[a]	-5.57[a]	-3.61[a]	-3.48[a]	-5.87[a]	-4.50[a]
9–11	-1.29[a]	-0.94[a]	-1.70[a]	-1.29[a]	-1.18[a]	-0.74[a]	-1.66[a]	-0.85[a]
12	—	—	—	—	—	—	—	—
13–15	0.69[a]	0.83[a]	0.63[a]	0.50[a]	0.60[a]	0.80[a]	0.51[b]	0.45[a]
16	1.20[a]	1.23[a]	0.19	0.28	0.61[a]	1.01[a]	-1.06[a]	-0.10
17	1.30[a]	1.30[a]	-0.92[b]	-0.01	0.99[a]	1.08[a]	-0.96[c]	0.71[c]
18 and over	0.95[a]	1.12[a]	-1.12[b]	0.15	1.41[a]	1.48[a]	0.33	0.57
Constant	0.72	0.90	2.59	2.01	0.88	0.87	2.18	1.59
R^2	.43	.35	.52	.51	.40	.27	.59	.36
Mean age	41.00	38.50	39.30	38.30	40.10	36.90	39.40	37.80
Mean years of overeducation	-0.70	0.59	-1.34	0.38	0.00	0.72	-0.89	0.80
Number of observations	38,053	29,257	3,451	2,223	17,638	19,693	2,247	2,248

[a] Significant at .01 level.
[b] Significant at .05 level.
[c] Significant at .1 level.

81

FIGURE 4

Estimated Years of Overeducation by Schooling Level for the Employed Population by Race and Sex, 1960 and 1976

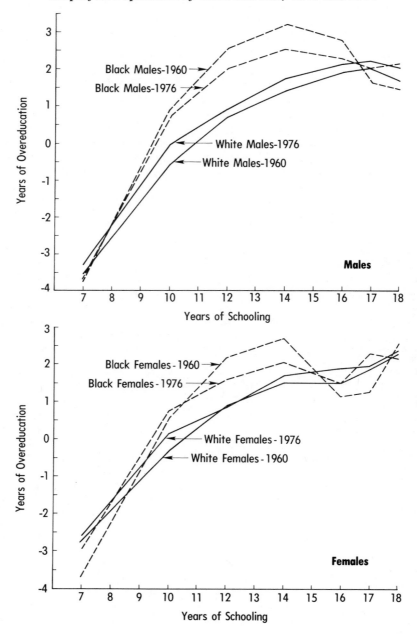

were more overeducated in 1976 than in 1960. The opposite situation occurred for black males; they were generally less overeducated for their jobs in 1976 than in 1980, although they remained more overeducated than white males. The only exception was black males with graduate training who were more overeducated in 1976 than in 1960. It is surprising that black males with graduate training in 1960 appeared less overeducated than their white male counterparts. This may have occurred because such a small number of black males completed graduate training that they were more likely to find jobs commensurate with their level of graduate training compared with whites. However, it is more difficult to make accurate statements concerning those workers with graduate training because some of that training is more specific in nature and therefore is unrelated to GED levels.

Differences between white and black females were similar to those between white and black males. White females were generally more overeducated in 1976 than in 1960, while black females were less overeducated in 1976 than in 1960. Differences varied for individuals with 16 or more years of schooling. Both white and black females with four years of college were more overeducated in 1976 than in 1960, yet black females continued to be less so than white females. White and black women with graduate training were similarly overeducated by 1976.

The preceding results on the incidence of overeducation within the working population can now be summarized. In the aggregate, the incidence of overeducation between 1960 and 1976 increased owing to small changes in the skill requirements of jobs and significant increases in the educational attainments of the working population. There were differences in these discrepancies among race and sex groups. Blacks, in general, held fewer jobs requiring high-skill levels; at the same time, they possessed lower levels of education than did whites. White males appeared to be the best-off; they held a higher percentage of the most-skilled jobs and possessed higher educational skills than workers from other groups. When years of overeducation are estimated by schooling level within each group, blacks are more overeducated for their jobs than whites. Between 1960 and 1976 the gap diminished. Blacks were less overeducated in 1976 than in 1960, while whites were more overeducated. The only exception to this relationship was workers with graduate training; whether white or black, they were generally more overeducated in 1976 than in 1960.

The Incidence of Overeducation
among Inexperienced Workers

The preceding evidence suggests that the incidence of overeducation has increased since 1960, in part, because of sharp increases in educational attainments among the working population. Since younger, inexperienced workers have completed more education, on the average, than older workers, it is likely that they also display higher incidences of overeducation. The following evidence tests this conjecture. The incidence of overeducation for the inexperienced working population is examined in the same manner as for the working population as a whole. First, a comparison is made of the aggregate distributions of skill requirements of the jobs held by this group with their equivalent levels of educational attainments; then, a disaggregation is made of these distributions by race and sex; finally, an analysis is made of the relationship between the years of overeducation and the years of schooling.

Table 11 shows the aggregate distribution of skill requirements for jobs held by the inexperienced working population as reflected by GED levels for 1960 and 1976. Equivalent years of schooling are also displayed based on the same two conversion systems that were used earlier. These results are displayed graphically in Figure 5. They

TABLE 11

Distribution of GED Levels and Educational Attainments for the
Inexperienced Employed Population, 1960 and 1976

Level	GED	Educational Attainments	
		I	II
1960			
1	3.1	0.1	0.0
2	14.6	2.9	0.9
3	40.8	22.0	7.2
4	26.9	48.0	64.9
5	10.7	22.9	12.1
6	3.3	4.1	14.9
1976			
1	1.8	0.0	0.0
2	17.9	1.3	0.1
3	35.6	16.8	4.7
4	27.6	42.8	56.1
5	14.1	33.0	16.5
6	2.8	6.0	22.6

Note: Educational attainments grouped into categories corresponding to equivalencies shown in Table 4. Percentage distributions may not add to 100.0 because of rounding.

FIGURE 5

Distribution of GED Levels and Educational Attainments for the
Inexperienced Employed Population, 1960 and 1976

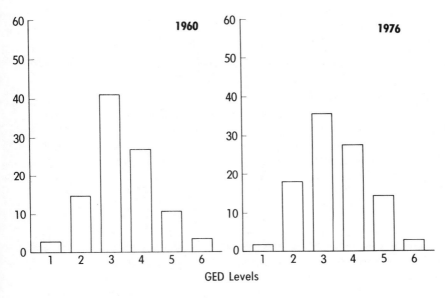

GED Levels

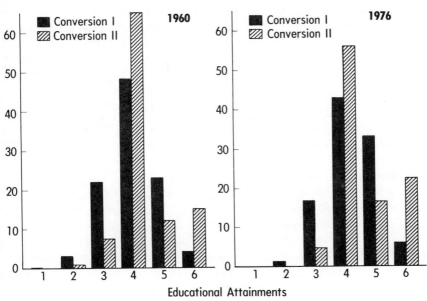

Educational Attainments

show similar patterns to those generated for the working population as a whole; that is, the skill requirements of jobs changed relatively little in the period between 1960 and 1976, while educational attainments increased substantially. Similarly, comparisons based on the second conversion system result in more glaring disparities between skill requirements and educational attainments than comparisons based on conversion I.

These estimates suggest that inexperienced workers are more educated than workers in general. For example, 39 percent of inexperienced workers in 1976 had completed some college (levels 5 and 6) compared with less than a third (32.6 percent) for the entire working population. Inexperienced workers also held a smaller percentage of the more-skilled jobs in the economy: 16.9 percent of the jobs they held in 1976 had skill requirements corresponding to GED levels 5 and 6 as compared with 19.7 percent for the working population as a whole. Thus, among inexperienced workers, over 56 percent of those with some college education were overeducated for their jobs in 1976, compared with 40 percent for the total employed population.

How do these results vary by race and sex? Table 12 shows the distribution of skill requirements for jobs held by inexperienced workers, disaggregated by race and sex, together with equivalent years of schooling. The results show that inexperienced white males held a higher percentage of the most-skilled jobs (GED level 6) in the economy relative to other inexperienced workers, although less than did white males in the entire working population. Yet, the percentage of inexperienced white males holding those jobs declined between 1960 and 1976, while the percentage of those jobs held by other inexperienced workers rose during the same period. Inexperienced blacks, in general, made significant advances in the percentage of skilled jobs that they held between 1960 and 1976. Black females, especially, increased their representation in the better jobs. By 1976 almost one-fifth (19.6 percent) of inexperienced black females held jobs at the second highest skill level (GED level 5), much more than any other group. Inexperienced males, both white and black, continued to hold a higher percentage of low-skilled jobs in 1976 than did inexperienced females.

Educational attainments rose between 1960 and 1976 for all inexperienced workers. White males continued to be better represented in the highest educational category (level 6). Within the two highest educational categories (levels 5 and 6), white and black females were as well represented as white males, with black males not as well represented. Both black males and black females registered the largest gains in educational attainments between 1960 and 1976. Inexperienced workers of each race and sex exhibited higher levels of educational attainment than did their counterparts in the entire working population, as was expected.

TABLE 12

Distribution of GED Levels and Educational Attainments for the
Inexperienced Employed Population by Race and Sex, 1960 and 1976

	Males				Females			
	White		Black		White		Black	
Level	1960	1976	1960	1976	1960	1976	1960	1976
GED levels								
1	3.7	2.6	9.4	4.9	1.2	0.8	6.1	1.4
2	18.3	24.1	32.1	30.0	6.7	10.2	18.9	14.0
3	37.3	29.8	41.7	32.3	45.1	42.3	51.3	40.6
4	23.8	26.8	12.0	21.8	34.0	29.2	14.7	22.8
5	10.9	12.6	3.0	8.8	11.5	15.7	8.6	19.6
6	5.0	3.9	0.7	2.0	1.4	1.7	0.6	1.5
Educational attainments								
1 (0–4)	0.0	0.0	0.9	0.0	0.0	0.0	0.0	0.0
2 (5–7)	3.4	1.5	12.7	2.0	1.0	1.2	3.4	0.5
3 (8–10)	25.0	17.8	33.7	21.1	16.5	15.9	21.1	10.8
4 (11–12)	42.2	40.8	41.8	51.1	56.6	44.5	55.2	48.3
5 (13–16)	23.5	32.3	9.5	21.6	23.7	34.1	19.4	35.4
6 (17–18)	5.8	7.6	1.4	4.2	2.2	4.3	0.9	5.1

Note: Equivalent years of schooling (numbers in parentheses)
are based on conversion I, Table 4. Percentage distributions may
not add to 100.0 because of rounding.

Judging from disparities between educational attainments and
the skill requirements of jobs held by inexperienced workers, the incidence of overeducation is universal. Black females exhibit the
greatest relative discrepancy between educational attainments and the
skill requirements of their jobs at the highest level (6)—5.1 percent
versus 1.5 percent, respectively. Within the two highest categories
(levels 5 and 6), all inexperienced workers show a substantial discrepancy between their educational attainments and the skill requirements of their jobs.

These relationships are further illustrated in the regression estimates predicting years of overeducation by schooling level for inexperienced workers. The results are displayed in Table 13. As with
the previous regression results, education is represented by dummy

TABLE 13

Estimated Years of Overeducation by Schooling Level for the Inexperienced Employed Population by Race and Sex, 1960 and 1976

| | Males | | | | Females | | | |
| | White | | Black | | White | | Black | |
	1960	1976	1960	1976	1960	1976	1960	1976
Years of schooling								
0–8	-3.44^a	-2.69^a	-4.52^a	-3.22^a	-3.00^a	-3.18^a	-4.53^a	-2.89^a
9–11	-0.97^a	-0.76^a	-1.71^a	-1.25^a	-0.93^a	-0.78^a	-1.69^a	-1.10^a
12	—	—	—	—	—	—	—	—
13–15	0.29^a	0.75^a	0.96^b	0.24	0.89^a	0.98^a	0.48	0.52^a
16	-0.06	0.55^a	-0.40	-0.31	0.33^a	0.78^a	-1.34^a	-0.15
17	0.33	0.53^a	-1.19	-1.28^c	1.44^a	1.02^a	-1.64	0.13
18 and over	-0.21	0.39^a	-1.14	-0.04	1.03^b	1.14^a	0.76	0.27
Constant	1.83	1.98	3.18	2.60	1.07	1.22	2.67	1.83
R^2	.18	.13	.47	.14	.22	.21	.36	.09
Mean age	20.20	20.80	19.30	20.70	20.00	20.50	20.50	21.40
Mean years of overeducation	1.25	1.91	1.61	2.05	0.91	1.26	1.71	1.64
Number of observations	4,422	6,001	347	403	3,008	5,285	232	435

[a]Significant at .01 level.
[b]Significant at .05 level.
[c]Significant at .1 level.

FIGURE 6

Estimated Years of Overeducation by Schooling Level for the
Inexperienced Employed Population by Race and Sex, 1960 and 1976

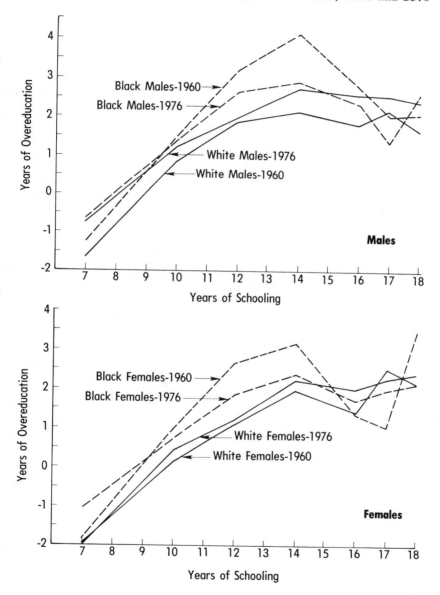

variables so that the values of the coefficients signify estimated years of overeducation by schooling level relative to the constant, which represents estimated years of overeducation for persons with 12 years of schooling. Figure 6 illustrates estimated years of overeducation by years of schooling for each race and sex group. Consistent with estimates of the entire working population, more-educated individuals exhibit a higher degree of overeducation than less-educated individuals. This relationship holds true for all groups. However, there are some significant differences among the groups. In general, inexperienced blacks are more overeducated for their jobs than inexperienced whites except at very high education levels. Inexperienced women, especially whites, with 12 years of schooling tend to be less overeducated than men with 12 years of schooling.

Even more interesting are the changes that took place among inexperienced workers between 1960 and 1976. In 1960 blacks with some college (13 to 15 years of schooling) were much more overeducated than similarly educated whites. By 1976 this disparity had diminished. Yet even in 1976 there tended to be a stronger "credential" effect (less overeducation for persons with four years of college than for persons with one to three years of college) among blacks than among whites. These relationships were also evident in the entire working population. Another unanticipated result was the change in the amount of variance explained for inexperienced blacks. For both sexes there was a great reduction in the amount of variance explained between the two years, but especially for black women. Between 1960 and 1976 inexperienced white males experienced a significant deterioration in the standing of highly educated workers relative to those with 12 years of schooling. Inexperienced white women, on the other hand, did not experience such significant changes. They were more overeducated than high school graduates in 1960 and continued to be so in 1976. This was also true for white women in the working population as a whole. Curiously, inexperienced black women with four years of college were less overeducated than high school graduates in 1960, but not in 1976. This, again, was true for black women in the working population generally.

In summary, the upward shift in years of overeducation that occurred among the entire working population also occurred among inexperienced workers. Whites generally continue to be better-off because they tend to be less overeducated for their jobs than blacks. Still, there have been some noticeable improvements in the relative position of blacks between 1960 and 1976, particularly among those with some college training.

PROJECTIONS TO 1985

The previous results indicate that the incidence of overeducation increased in the period between 1960 and 1976. It is useful to forecast the demand for skills and the supply of educational attainments at some future time in order to see whether this trend will continue. This section contains some projections for the year 1985 that may provide some idea of the likelihood of overeducation continuing.

First, consider the demand for skills. There is no way of knowing the exact skill requirements of particular jobs in the future, but government projections on employment provide an approximate picture. Table 14 shows the projected growth rates for major occupation groups to 1985 computed by the Bureau of Labor Statistics. The largest projected growth rates are among service workers, clerical workers, and professional workers. Recall from Table 6 that service and clerical occupations lie almost exclusively in the middle and lower ranges of skill requirements. For example, more than one-quarter (27.7 percent) of service jobs had skill requirements in the lower two GED categories (levels 1 and 2) in 1976. Of the total projected job openings in the period between 1976 and 1985 (45.9 million), about 40 percent will occur in clerical and service areas. Thus, the prospects for substantial increases in the number of high-skilled jobs appear dim.

These trends will affect the overall distribution of GED levels of jobs within the U.S. economy in 1985. The projected distribution of employment in 1985 (Table 15) and the distribution of GED levels within each major occupation group in 1976 based on fourth edition DOT estimates (Table 6) were used to forecast the distribution of GED levels in 1985. The results appear in Table 16. The estimated distribution appears quite similar to the one for 1976. This is due to the offsetting effects of growth in higher-skilled jobs (professional and managerial) versus middle- and lower-skilled jobs (clerical and service). Of course, these projections reflect neither changes in the skill requirements of individual jobs nor intraoccupational group shifts in employment. If the changes that took place in the period between 1960 and 1976 were to occur similarly in this future period, there may be a further reduction in skill requirements at the ends of the distribution. Proponents of job fragmentation would also argue that jobs will continue to be divided into lower-skilled components, resulting in intraoccupational group shifts toward lower-skilled jobs within each major category. But, of course, such conjectures will only be borne out by observing actual changes in the distribution of skill requirements as they occur.

Next, consider the supply of skills brought into the labor market. The educational attainments of the labor force are expected to rise in

TABLE 14

Employment and Job Openings by Occupation Group, 1976 and Projected 1985

(in thousands)

Occupation Group	1976 Employment	Projected 1985 Employment	Percent Change	Total Openings, 1976-85*
White-collar workers	43,700	53,500	22.4	24,800
Professional and technical workers	13,329	15,800	18.2	6,400
Managers and administrators	9,315	11,300	21.0	5,400
Sales workers	5,497	6,400	16.6	3,000
Clerical workers	15,558	20,000	28.8	10,000
Blue-collar workers	28,958	34,100	17.9	12,800
Craft and kindred workers	11,278	13,700	21.6	5,500
Operatives	13,356	15,600	16.9	5,800
Nonfarm laborers	4,325	4,800	11.3	1,600
Service workers	12,005	14,800	23.4	8,100
Private household workers	1,125	900	-18.8	500
Other service workers	10,880	13,900	27.7	7,600
Farm workers	2,822	1,900	-34.1	200
Total	87,485	104,300	19.2	45,900

*Openings are due to employment growth and the replacement of workers who die or retire.

Note: Details may not add to totals because of rounding.

Source: U.S., Bureau of Labor Statistics 1979b, p. 6.

92

TABLE 15

Distribution of Employment by Occupation Group,
1976 and Projected 1985

Occupation Group	1976	1985
White-collar workers	49.9	51.3
Professional and technical workers	15.2	15.1
Managers and administrators	10.6	10.8
Sales workers	6.3	6.1
Clerical workers	17.8	19.2
Blue-collar workers	33.1	32.7
Craft and kindred workers	12.9	13.2
Operatives	15.2	15.0
Nonfarm laborers	4.9	4.6
Service workers	13.7	14.2
Private household workers	1.3	0.9
Other service workers	12.4	13.3
Farm workers	3.2	1.8
Total	100.0	100.0

Note: Percentage distributions may not add to 100.0 because
of rounding.

Source: U.S., Bureau of Labor Statistics (1979b), p. 5.

the future (Figure 7). For one thing, the college-age population is
expected to continue to grow during this period (Golladay 1977, p.
146). The other determining factor is the participation rate of this
group. While some have argued that the participation rate will decline as labor market opportunities diminish (Freeman 1976), it is
unclear that this will happen. For example, the educational participation rate among older workers (35 years and older) has grown
quite dramatically in recent years (Golladay 1977, p. 226). Even if
the participation rate fails to increase, or even decreases, during this
period, the educational attainments of the labor force will rise as
older, less-educated workers are displaced by younger, more-educated workers.

Again, government projections were used to make a rough estimate of the expected discrepancy between GED levels and equivalent
years of schooling in the year 1985 (Table 16). The distributions of
educational attainments shown in Table 16 only approximate the equiva-

TABLE 16

Distribution of GED and Education Levels, 1976 and Projected 1985

Level	Equivalent Years of Schooling[a]	GED		Educational Attainments	
		1976	1985	1976	1985[b]
1	0-4	1.6	1.7	1.8	0.9
2	5-7	13.2	12.8	4.1	2.4
3	8-10	29.8	25.7	16.8	19.7[c]
4	11-12	35.4	40.2	44.7	40.7[d]
5	13-16	16.1	15.8	25.8	28.1
6	17-18	3.6	3.7	6.8	8.1

[a]From Table 4, conversion I.
[b]Data in this column are taken from U.S., Bureau of Labor Statistics (1974b, p. 25).
[c]Corresponds to 8 to 11 years of schooling.
[d]Corresponds to 12 years of schooling.

Note: Percentage distributions may not add to 100.0 because of rounding.

FIGURE 7

Educational Attainments of the Labor Force, 1957-90

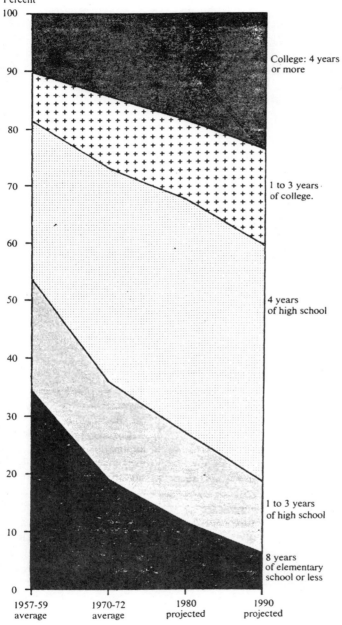

Percent

College: 4 years
or more

1 to 3 years
of college.

4 years
of high school

1 to 3 years
of high school

8 years
of elementary
school or less

1957-59
average

1970-72
average

1980
projected

1990
projected

Source: Golladay 1976, p. 120.

95

lencies used previously. Nonetheless, they indicate a growing incidence of overeducation by 1985. For example, only one-fifth of the jobs in 1985 will require a college education (GED levels 5 and 6), about the same proportion as in 1976. Meanwhile, more than a third (36.3 percent) of the working population is projected to have completed some college by that time.

These figures suggest that the incidence of overeducation is likely to persist in the future as a result of little or no projected change in the distribution of skills required for jobs in the face of rising educational attainments for the working population.

SUMMARY

This chapter examined the incidence of overeducation in the U.S. labor market. Estimates were based on observed discrepancies between the educational attainments of the working population and the skill requirements of their jobs in the years 1960 and 1976. Skill requirements were indexed by levels of General Educational Development (GED) estimated by the U.S. Employment Service.

The analysis of overeducation was performed in several parts. The first part examined changes in the skill requirements of jobs. Despite the growth in higher-skilled professional, technical, and managerial employment during this period, there was a net decrease in the percentage of the working population holding jobs at the highest skill level (GED level 6). This finding was totally unexpected. There were increases at the other higher-skill levels (GED levels 4 and 5), however, and decreases in the proportion of jobs held requiring low levels of skills (GED levels 1-3).

The second part examined the changes in educational attainments of the working population during this same period. The results were not surprising—educational attainments rose appreciably between 1960 and 1976.

The third part examined the incidence of overeducation by contrasting skill requirements of jobs with educational attainments. To make these comparisons, skill requirements were first translated into equivalent years of schooling using two different conversions that were introduced in the previous chapter. Comparisons were performed on two groups, the total working population and the inexperienced working population. For these two groups, aggregate comparisons were made first, then comparisons by race and sex groups, followed by estimates of years of overeducation by schooling level. For the working population as a whole, the incidence of overeducation increased in the period between 1960 and 1976. This was due to minor changes in the skill requirements of jobs and sharp increases in the educational attainments of the working population. This relationship held for whites and blacks, males and females. In general, blacks continued to be more overeducated for their jobs than whites in 1976 as in 1960, although these differences diminished during this period. For all groups, those with the most schooling showed the highest degree of overeducation.

The results for the inexperienced working population were similar. But because inexperienced workers had higher levels of educational attainment than workers in the entire working population, they tended to be even more overeducated. Again, this was true for all race and sex groups, although the disparities between whites and blacks were not so great as in the working population as a whole.

The last part of this research projected the incidence of overeducation for the year 1985 using figures on projected employment and educational attainment. These results indicate that overeducation will persist in the future unless there are either significant changes in the skill requirements of jobs or large drops in educational participation. Either occurrence appears unlikely.

What do these results show? First, they indicate that a condition of overeducation, as defined in this part of the study, has existed in the labor market for some time. Others have also found this to be true (Miller 1971; Lucas 1972; Berg, Freedman, and Freeman 1978). Moreover, the amount of overeducation rises with years of schooling. This means that overeducation does not simply affect highly educated workers. Even workers with a high school education hold jobs incommensurate with their level of training. The second major finding is that the incidence of overeducation increased in the period between 1960 and 1976. This resulted from two factors: a lack of change in the general skill requirements of jobs together with the rising educational attainments of the working population. Third, the incidence of overeducation varies among different race and sex groups. Blacks are generally more overeducated than whites, although their situation improved during this period. More important, the position of inexperienced workers worsened relative to the working population as a whole. In particular, college graduates (four years of college) in all four groups were worse-off in 1976 than they were in 1960. This finding substantiates the general observation that college graduates are not faring well in the contemporary labor market. Finally, projections for the future indicate that the incidence of overeducation is likely to increase. This suggests that overeducation, which has existed for some time in the labor market, will persist and may even grow.

These results should not be viewed as definitive. Educational attainments signify more than simply general skills. Furthermore, as the discussion in Chapter 1 pointed out, there is no universally accepted meaning for the word overeducation. The definition used in this empirical investigation is only one of several alternative possibilities. In addition, there are a number of methodological difficulties in measuring overeducation when it is based on the discrepancies between educational attainments and the skill requirements of jobs. As a result, the findings presented here must be considered tentative. Nonetheless, it is hard to escape the conclusion that a condition of overeducation exists in the labor market, at least according to the definition used here.

The final part of this study addresses itself to the implications of overeducation for the workplace and for public and private policy. As in the first part of the study, overeducation is considered in several ways rather than according to a specific definition.

NOTES

1. The term <u>working population</u> will be used repeatedly throughout this chapter in reference to those respondents in the 1960 and 1976 data files—individuals, 14 years old and over, who were employed at the time of the census surveys.

2. For a more detailed analysis of skill changes in this period, see Rumberger (forthcoming).

3. However, the actual distributions they produced only roughly correspond to the ones presented here because of the different methodologies employed in assigning GED levels to census occupation codes.

PART III
IMPLICATIONS

5

IMPLICATIONS OF OVEREDUCATION
IN THE WORKPLACE

INTRODUCTION

Overeducation is more than an academic concern. It has received considerable attention, in part, because it is thought to have
potentially disruptive and adverse consequences in the workplace.
For instance, the U.S. Department of Health, Education and Welfare
report, Work in America, discusses the problems of U.S. working
life, including those that result from integrating young, better educated workers into the job hierarchy. Business leaders worry that
at least some of their current labor problems stem from the increasing numbers of highly educated workers entering the labor force. [1]
These concerns warrant some attention. Are there adverse consequences of overeducation in the workplace? This chapter will attempt
to answer this question. If adverse effects do exist, it could have important implications for firms employing overeducated workers.
Furthermore, government policy may need to address this condition
as a social problem. A discussion of the implications of overeducation for public and private policy occurs in the final chapter of this
study.

This chapter is divided into two parts. The first part explores
some possible consequences of overeducation that could logically
arise in the workplace. The discussion includes some potential causal
relationships that may tie these conditions together. The second part
examines the empirical support that exists in the literature to substantiate the proposed relationships. In general, little direct empirical support exists to verify these relationships. Consequently, the
discussion highlights those areas needing further research.

A number of problems, both conceptual and methodological,
make the proposed tasks of this chapter difficult. First, there are

a host of possible factors, in addition to overeducation, that influence conditions in the workplace making it hard to distinguish between the effects of overeducation and the effects of other factors. Second, the causal relationships among the various factors are often unclear, compounding the difficulty of tracing the effects to any single factor. Furthermore, the effects of overeducation may be indirect; observed consequences in the workplace may result from its effects on such underlying psychological variables as motivation or expectations. Finally, an analysis of the effects of overeducation can be made from more than one perspective. Most of the available literature takes an individualistic perspective, examining how individuals fit into their various work roles based on their particular characteristics, using psychological measures of behavior and attitudes. The present discussion will restrict itself to such a perspective. However, a different framework, which is emobdied in a Marxist perspective, examines the conditions of work and the experiences of workers as a class. A discussion based on this perspective is deferred until the next chapter.

Chapter 1 reviewed three possible definitions of overeducation. Overeducation may be defined as a decline in the economic position of educated individuals relative to historically higher levels, as unrealized expectations of the educated (either in an absolute or relative sense) with respect to characteristics of their work (such as, pay, prestige, challenge), or as the possession by workers of greater educational skills than their jobs require. Although each of these forms of overeducation could conceivably have adverse effects in the workplace, it is the latter two that are the most likely to have an impact. For example, job dissatisfaction is unlikely to arise simply because a new college graduate today earns less, on the average, than a new college graduate earned five years ago. Dissatisfaction could arise because one's expectations remain unfulfilled in the job (such as an expectation about salary) or because one's educational skills are not being fully utilized.

Overeducation could lead to a variety of individual responses. These can be classified into four types: effects on attitudes, health (mental and physical), behavior, and performance. These responses are illustrated in Figure 8, together with the possible internal linkages between them. Overeducation could evoke each response, directly or indirectly, through its effects on other areas. For example, it is plausible that overeducation could affect workers' performance by promoting feelings of dissatisfaction that, in turn, could affect performance. Poor work performance could, on the other hand, simply be a symptom of the psychological effect of overeducation on motivation. In the latter view, overeducation influences simultaneously both workers' attitudes and performance. All the linkages shown in the diagram may not actually exist, but all are plausible. These linkages

FIGURE 8

The Possible Effects of Overeducation in the Workplace

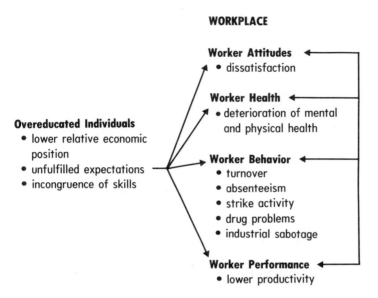

WORKPLACE

and the underlying variables are discussed in more detail shortly. First, it is worth speculating about the consequences of overeducation that may arise.

Overeducation, defined either as unrealized expectations or as a discrepancy between workers' skills and the skills required in their jobs, could promote feelings of job dissatisfaction. In the first instance, dissatisfaction could arise because of feelings of disappointment or frustration. Overeducated individuals may believe that they deserve jobs of higher pay, prestige, or autonomy than they actually received given their level of education. Although it could be argued that feelings of dissatisfaction arising from unrealized expectations may diminish over time as workers adjust to their situations, there is no apparent reason why that should be the case.[2] Outward signs of dissatisfaction may subside as individuals resign themselves to the realities of their jobs, but these feelings could be internalized, resulting in long-term effects on their mental health.

Dissatisfaction could also arise from the second type of overeducation. Individuals may find their needs for such things as challenge, autonomy, or self-fulfillment in their jobs left unsatisfied. They may be unable to fulfill these needs because they are stuck in narrowly structured jobs that do not demand full use of their skills. The dissatisfaction that results may actually increase over time as these individuals master the duties of their jobs and become increasingly frustrated (Kallenberg and Sorenson 1973).

In a similar manner, overeducation could produce other effects: deteriorated mental and physical health, declines in productivity, and increased incidences of absenteeism, industrial sabotage, drug problems, turnover, and strike activity. For example, the discrepancy between workers' skills and those required in their jobs could lead to declines in productivity as well as feelings of job dissatisfaction. If individuals feel that their skills are underutilized in their jobs and their needs unfulfilled, then their motivation may deteriorate to a point where they stop trying or caring about their work. Consequently, their productivity would decline. Motivation and performance could similarly be affected by unfulfilled expectations.

Because of the vast array of intervening factors and the general complexity of the proposed relationships, little direct evidence exists to substantiate these conjectures. For this reason, there is also little merit in analyzing aggregate trends on the incidence of these conditions since the effects of overeducation may be compounded by other factors that have changed over time. For example, after analyzing aggregate data on job satisfaction between 1963 and 1973, Quinn, Staines, and McCullough (1974, p. 6) conclude that there was no significant change in the observed level of job satisfaction during this period. Conversely, Andrisani et al. (1977) found a slight decline in job satisfaction since 1966 based on data from the National Longitudinal Surveys.[3]

These conflicting results demonstrate an inherent weakness in citing aggregate changes: they may hide the effects of numerous offsetting trends. Aggregate changes, for instance, are affected by cyclic variations in the economy. One would not expect the same consequences of overeducation, particularly increased turnover, in a time of high unemployment as in one of low unemployment where there are more opportunities for changing jobs. Although it has been shown that overeducation increased during the early 1970s, this was also a period of sharp economic downturn (declining real growth rates and rising unemployment rates). Thus, there may be no observed increase in worker dissatisfaction or other adverse behavior when those potentially negative effects are mediated by unfavorable labor market conditions.

With these qualifications in mind, the remainder of this chapter examines the empirical evidence on individual responses to overeducation. Although there are few studies that have directly studied the effects of overeducation, there is an extensive literature that discusses the nature of these various workplace conditions generally.[4]

By examining this literature it may be possible to draw some inferences about these proposed relationships.

OVEREDUCATION AND JOB DISSATISFACTION

   Part of the difficulty with assessing the influence of overeducation on job satisfaction arises from the complexity of the concept of
job satisfaction itself. Although considerable research has been undertaken on the subject during the last 50 years, there still remains
considerable debate over what it means, how to measure it, and what
factors influence it (see Vroom 1964). Some suggest that any unidi-
mensional index of satisfaction is inadequate since there are a number
of aspects of a job with which a worker may be dissatisfied and which,
in turn, could enter into an overall assessment of job satisfaction
(Quinn, Staines, and McCullough 1974). Others point out that different aspects of jobs may influence satisfaction and dissatisfaction.
The absence of a factor that normally promotes job dissatisfaction
may not lead to job satisfaction (Herzberg, Mausner, and Snyderman
1959). For example, raising a worker's salary may reduce job dissatisfaction, but not make a worker more satisfied. Satisfaction may
depend upon receiving intrinsic rewards from work.
   Despite these complexities, a number of studies have examined
the relationship between overeducation and job satisfaction directly.
Some of these defined overeducation as the underutilization of educational skills. Kalleberg and Sorensen (1973) found a significant relationship between overeducation defined in this manner and worker
dissatisfaction, although the amount of explained variance was low.
Quinn and Mandilovitch (1975) found a nonlinear relationship between
the absolute levels of educational attainment and job satisfaction but
a significant relationship between the relative levels of workers' education and their job satisfaction. They contrasted each worker's level
of education relative to what the worker thought was required in the
job, what the Employment Service said was required (GED level),
and the mean educational level of others in the worker's immediate
work group. In each case, relative education was a significant pre-
dictor of job satisfaction, with those most overeducated for their jobs
reporting the most dissatisfaction (pp. 27-28). Finally, Berg (1970),
using information on blue-collar workers, constructed a status inconsistency scale that measured the discrepancy between workers' education levels and the skills required in their jobs. Again, the most
dissatisfied workers had more education than was required in their
jobs.
   There is also some direct evidence to support the notion that
overeducation promotes dissatisfaction, where overeducation is de-

fined in terms of unfulfilled expectations for promotions. Berg (1970), using the same data, found that the consequences of status inconsistency were affected by expectations for promotion. Those with high status inconsistency (high education and low-skilled jobs) were more dissatisfied if they held jobs in which there was little perceived change of being promoted (p. 129). Berg also argues that the effects of these unfulfilled expectations are mediated by the treatment of those in similar situations, what he calls relative deprivation. In those industries where there were few persons with status inconsistency, persons of high status inconsistency felt more dissatisfied than persons in industries where there were large numbers of workers with status inconsistency. This suggests that individuals may evaluate their positions relative to those around them.

These results are by no means sufficient to prove that overeducation results in job dissatisfaction, but they are suggestive. In addition, there has been substantial research done on the topic of job satisfaction generally which may lend some indirect support for this proposed relationship.

Researchers have identified a number of factors that contribute to job satisfaction. They include the characteristics of individuals, the characteristics of the jobs that they occupy, and the match or congruence between these characteristics. Vroom (1964, p. 173) argues, in fact, that a thorough understanding of job satisfaction can only result from investigating the complex interaction among all the contributing factors. Job characteristics include the physical aspects of the job (salary, job content [tasks and autonomy], promotional possibilities) as well as the social aspects of the job (peers and supervisors). Job characteristics are, in turn, influenced by many factors, including the organization of the company in which the job exists and the company environment (Sutermeister 1976). The characteristics of individuals include needs, skills and abilities, aspirations and expectations, and personalities. There is an extensive literature that simply addresses the nature of the needs. For example, Maslow (1970) suggests a hierarchy of needs and argues that the lowest ones, such as food and shelter, must be fulfilled before the higher level needs, such as self-fulfillment. Some researchers believe that workers today are interested primarily in fulfilling their social and egoistic needs from work since most jobs are able to fulfill their physical needs for such things as comfort and safety (Sutermeister 1976, pp. 90–91). Vroom (1964) suggests that individuals possess an array of needs, but they differ in the relative importance that they attach to each need. Some workers, for example, may have a stronger need for self-esteem while others have a stronger need for self-fulfillment. Individuals may fulfill some of their needs on the job and some away from the job.

Similarly, there are a number of factors that influence the characteristics of individuals. Most important, the characteristics of jobs interact with the characteristics of the individuals in the jobs. Not everyone may respond to the same job characteristics in the same manner because everyone has different needs and expectations (Kalleberg 1977).

Education may influence both the characteristics of individuals and the characteristics of their jobs. Flanagan, Strauss, and Ulman (1974) suggest that education increases workers' desires for nonpecuniary versus pecuniary benefits from work. Highly educated workers may become dissatisfied because they fail to find jobs with the mix of benefits they desire. Education, in this sense, may influence the needs that workers bring into their jobs or the expectations about their jobs given their level of education. Other findings support this notion. For example, recent studies indicate that more-educated workers have more interest in challenging work than financially rewarding work compared with less-educated individuals (Quinn and Mandilovitch 1975, pp. 44-53; Sheppard and Herrick 1972, p. 119). Education also helps individuals secure jobs that have desirable characteristics. Furthermore, research shows that certain characteristics of jobs (such as challenge and autonomy) are correlated with job satisfaction (Srivastva et al. 1977; Sheppard and Herrick 1972; Quinn and Mandilovitch 1975). Thus, more-educated individuals are more likely to have jobs that offer the characteristics they require to achieve satisfaction from their jobs.

It is possible to infer how overeducation influences job satisfaction by examining its effects on both the characteristics of individuals and the characteristics of their jobs. Two of the definitions of overeducation in this study are based on discrepancies between the characteristics of individuals and their jobs: one in terms of skills and the other in terms of expectations. There is some evidence that the discrepancy in skills could contribute to job dissatisfaction, although this literature did not link the formation of skills explicitly to education. Vroom (1964, pp. 142-44) reviews the evidence and concludes that individuals are more satisfied with their jobs if they are required to use the skills that they believe they possess. Bisconti and Solmon (1977), in their study of newly employed college graduates, find that job satisfaction can be predicted with a variable that measures whether respondents feel that their skills are underutilized in their current jobs.

Job dissatisfaction can also arise when expectations are not realized. Sheppard and Herrick (1972), in analyzing job dissatisfaction among young, white, blue-collar workers, find that a discrepancy between the importance a worker places on an aspect of work and the fulfillment of that aspect on the job (what they call an expectation gap) is related to job satisfaction. They conclude "that the important difference between the dissatisfaction of young workers and that of their elders stems, first, from the high value they placed on challenging work, and second, from the lack of challenge in the work they were actually required to perform" (p. 119). Vroom (1964, pp. 165-67), after reviewing the literature of experimental and social psychology, concludes that there is considerable support for the notion that job satisfaction is influenced by workers' expectations about the characteristics of their jobs. If these ideas are correct, then it is not so much what characteristics or rewards a job offers in any absolute sense, but rather, how these rewards measure up to what an individual expects. Expectations may only consist of a sense of fairness or equity, either in an absolute sense or relative to others with whom individuals compare themselves (Vroom 1964, pp. 167-72). Recent college graduates, for example, may feel that they deserve higher salaries or more challenging work relative to high school graduates.

To summarize, there is some direct evidence that overeducation leads to job dissatisfaction. The literature on the general relationship between education and job satisfaction adds further credence to this proposition. However, further research is needed to fully verify this proposed relationship.

OVEREDUCATION AND WORK PERFORMANCE

Overeducation may impair work performance. No direct evidence verifies this proposition, but a number of studies have examined the general relationship between education and performance. Berg (1970) reviewed several studies that were conducted on both blue-collar and white-collar workers. These studies do not test the hypothesis that overeducated workers perform poorly, but rather, they examine whether educational attainments (or credentials) contribute to effective performance. Berg concludes that the literature "has yielded little concrete evidence of a positive relationship between workers' educational achievements and their performance records in many work settings in the private sector" (p. 104). Diamond and Bedrosian (1970), in conjunction with the Department of Labor, undertook a study of employer hiring standards for a mixture of ten white-collar and blue-collar jobs in two metropolitan areas. The hiring standards included age, sex, education, and work experience. They conclude that "the characteristics and qualifications of employees which employers required or preferred showed little relationship to job performance" (p. 5). Although by no means conclusive, these results suggest that education may not serve as a good indicator of effective job performance.

As in the case of job dissatisfaction, one can infer how overeducation affects job performance by understanding the nature of job performance, in general, and the factors that influence it. Next to job satisfaction, job performance is one of the most studied topics in industrial psychology. One reason is quite apparent: businesses have long been concerned with how to maximize the performance of their workers. As a result, there has been a host of studies on this subject. Researchers who have investigated job performance generally agree that it is both a function of the ability of the workers and their motivation to perform (Sutermeister 1976; Vroom 1964). Performance could be limited by a lack of motivation even if an individual possesses the requisite ability to perform a job; performance could also be limited by a lack of ability even if the individual has the required motivation to perform the job. Overeducation implies that an individual has the requisite ability to perform adequately in the job. What is of most concern, therefore, is understanding how overeducation could affect employee motivation.

This task becomes difficult since the relationship between worker motivation and job performance is rather unclear. It is often assumed that there is a positive and linear relationship between the two, that performance increases monotonically with an individual's motivation. Vroom (1964) points out, however, that this assumption may be invalid. He reviews research that shows how performance may actually decline as the amount of motivation increases. This suggests that the relationship between motivation and performance is more complex than is often assumed.

Nonetheless, researchers have linked a number of factors to worker motivation (Porter and Lawler 1968; Vroom 1964; Sutermeister 1976). These factors include the physical aspects of the job, the social aspects of the job, and the personality traits and abilities of the individual holding the job. As in the case of job satisfaction, it is most important to consider the interaction of these factors as well as each one individually (Vroom 1964, p. 262). Research has found that workers perform more effectively if they perceive that their performance is rewarded (Vroom 1964; Porter and Lawler 1968). In this case performance is a means to some desired end. Performance may also be an end in itself, independent of the rewards tied to effective performance (Vroom 1964).[5]

One can infer from this literature how overeducation may affect job performance. Vroom (1964) shows how workers are motivated to perform if they believe that effective performance depends upon their abilities. Overeducated workers may believe that they have many abilities that are unrelated to effective performance in their jobs. Consequently, they may lose motivation. Vroom also reviews research on the effects of wages on motivation. He concludes that "workers strive to maximize the equity of their wages and attempt to perform at a level which is most consistent with their conceptions of the relative rates and qualifications of themselves and their co-workers" (p. 255, emphasis in the original). This reasoning suggests that overeducated workers, because they feel that their wages are inequitable for the qualifications they possess, may not be motivated in their jobs. Although the literature does not test these conjectures directly, they are consistent with the existing evidence.

Overeducation, through its effects on factors like job satisfaction, may also influence job performance indirectly. Overeducation may impair job performance because it produces job dissatisfaction. The relationship between job satisfaction and job performance has been studied widely. It is often assumed that high levels of job satisfaction will lead to high levels of job performance and, conversely, that low levels of job satisfaction will lead to poor job performance. Sutermeister (1976, pp. 46-49) argues that high or low job satisfaction may lead to either high or low job performance. Most researchers agree that the relationship between job satisfaction and performance is highly complex and that a number of factors may mediate this relationship. [6] Nevertheless, a positive but weak relationship between the two has been substantiated by a number of researchers (Slocum 1970; Lawler and Porter 1967; Srivastva et al. 1977). This positive association, which does not explain causality, may result from a set of factors simultaneously influencing both performance and job satisfaction. In fact, Lawler and Porter (1967) suggest that effective performance probably leads to job satisfaction rather than the other way around.

In summary, overeducation may lead to poor job performance although no evidence supports such a claim directly. But a review of the factors that affect job performance does at least suggest that overeducated workers may exhibit poor job performance due to low motivation on the job.

OVEREDUCATION AND WORKER HEALTH

Overeducation may also have degrading effects on the physical and mental health of workers. Most research concentrates on mental health, although evidence does suggest that there may be adverse physical effects from some mental conditions, such as stress, that can result from job dissatisfaction (House 1974; Margolis and Kroes 1974).

Again, because of the vast array of factors that influence health, there is no direct evidence to substantiate this proposition. The plausibility may be strengthened by reviewing the nature of health generally and the factors on the job that may influence it. As with the other workplace conditions, a number of methodological and conceptual issues surround the study of workers' health. Most important, there is the issue of what constitutes an accurate measure of health. The condition of physical health is easier to determine than the condition of mental health. There are a number of measures of mental health, including functional effectiveness, general well-being, and psychiatric symptoms (Kasl 1974, p. 172). Furthermore, these indexes are interrelated.

Most explanatory frameworks for understanding mental health are complex (Kasl 1974; Kornhauser 1965). Normally, they include the influences of job characteristics, worker characteristics, and the interaction between the two sets of factors. Kornhauser, however, suggests that the effects of job characteristics and individual characteristics act independently on mental health. For example, he finds strong differences in the mental health of workers by occupational level, with those in the most skilled occupations exhibiting the best mental health. But the problem remains of attributing these differences to the job characteristics themselves or the characteristics of the people that occupy those types of jobs. Kasl (1974) points out that differences in job status may, in fact, be attributable to systematic differences in job involvement between those in various occupations. Furthermore, these general tendencies may be mediated by other individual differences, such as influences outside the job.

What Kornhauser attributes to job characteristics alone may actually be related to the discrepancy between the characteristics of jobs and the characteristics of individuals in those jobs. For example, in trying to determine the factors that contribute to mental health differences by occupation, Kornhauser finds in his study of factory workers that "workers' feelings regarding the use of their abilities is unmistakably associated with the superior mental health of the group of higher factory jobs and the poorer mental health at low job levels" (p. 99). He adds that a lack of use of one's abilities may lead to poor mental health by

> causing lower self-esteem, discouragement, futility, and feelings of failure and inferiority in contrast to a sense of personal growth and self-fulfillment resulting from more varied, responsible, challenging undertakings that afford opportunity to develop and use one's ideas and skills.
> [P. 129]

Other studies support the notion that a discrepancy between workers' skills and the skills of their jobs may result in a deterioration in mental health (Gardell 1976; Coburn 1975).

This literature fails to address the influence of education on mental health. By giving individuals other avenues through which to maintain their well-being, education may mediate the potentially negative effects of highly educated workers in low-level jobs (Kornhauser 1965, pp. 136-37). Kornhauser did find that better educated workers in low-level jobs exhibited low levels of life satisfaction and self-esteem (p. 137).

Researchers also acknowledge that unrealized expectations on the job may lead to frustrations that impair self-esteem and, consequently, lower overall mental health (Kornhauser 1965, p. 155; Kasl 1974, p. 186). Critics may argue that the effects of these unrealized expectations become shortlived as such workers modify their expectations and aspirations. But Kornhauser states that

> the unsatisfactory mental health of working people consists of no small measure of their dwarfed desires and deadened initiative, reduction of goals and restriction of their efforts to a point where life is relatively empty and only half meaningful. [P. 270]

Finally, overeducation may affect workers' mental health through its effect on job satisfaction. Job satisfaction is sometimes used as one index of mental health and, as mentioned earlier, the various indexes of mental health are interrelated. As with the previous workplace conditions, it appears more likely that a complex interaction between job and individual characteristics affects simultaneously both job satisfaction and mental health. Yet, both effects may not be observed to the same degree. Overeducation may result in job dissatisfaction but not poor mental health, because the latter condition may be strongly influenced by factors outside the job.

In summary, most researchers propose a complex model to explain mental health, accounting for both individual and job-related factors. Such a framework supports the possibility that overeducation may lead to a deterioration in workers' mental health. In fact, Kornhauser's major conclusion is that mental health problems may arise from the discrepancy between personal and job characteristics. This coincides with two definitions of overeducation, one based on skills and the other based on expectations. Of course, direct empirical verification is required to substantiate these propositions.

OVEREDUCATION AND ADVERSE WORKPLACE BEHAVIOR

Finally, overeducation may lead to disruptive workplace behavior such as increased incidences of turnover, absenteeism, strike activity, drug problems, or industrial sabotage. Again, there is no direct evidence to support this proposition. A review of the available research on workplace behavior does suggest, however, how these adverse effects could result from overeducation. Most of this literature focuses on turnover and absenteeism (collectively referred to as withdrawal behavior), with only a few studies addressing the issues of strike activity, industrial sabotage, and drug problems. [7]

Again, an array of conceptual and methodological issues surrounds the study of workplace behavior (Pettman 1975). The study of workplace behavior is further compounded by the influence of the external labor market, including such macroeconomic conditions as the level of unemployment. As mentioned earlier, one would not expect similar workplace behavior under different conditions in the external labor market. Overeducation, for example, is more likely to increase job turnover when the unemployment rate is low (when there are more alternative opportunities for employment) than when it is high. More caution is required, therefore, in generalizing from research that fails to account for external labor market conditions.

The literature on turnover and absenteeism deals primarily with the relationship between these behaviors and job satisfaction. [8] Most evidence suggests a negative relationship between job satisfaction and worker turnover, with dissatisfied workers displaying higher incidences of turnover. There is a similar, though weaker, consensus on a negative relationship between job satisfaction and absenteeism. After reviewing 29 studies, Nicholson, Brown, and Chadwick-Jones (1976) conclude that there is insubstantial evidence that job dissatisfaction fosters absenteeism. The study of job satisfaction and absenteeism may be more prone to methodological problems. Perhaps the influence of job satisfaction on absenteeism is more often mediated by other factors, while the influence of job satisfaction on turnover is not.

Quinn and his colleagues also analyzed the relationship between job satisfaction and self-reported incidences of industrial sabotage (theft and property damage) and drug usage. They found that job dissatisfaction significantly predicted both industrial sabotage and drug usage, although the relationship was most pronounced among men 30 years old and older (Quinn and Sheppard 1974, pp. 259-61; Mangione and Quinn 1975). Perhaps younger workers, because they still harbor expectations of mobility, are less inclined to resort to these behaviors than older workers who see less likelihood of advancement.

In summary, there is no direct support for the proposition that overeducation results in an increased incidence of adverse workplace behavior. Yet Porter and Steers (1973, p. 156) conclude that "these studies fairly consistently pointed out the importance of perceived equity and met expectations as important forces" in withdrawal decisions. Katz (1954) argues that industrial conflict is caused by many factors, one of which is workers' perceived deprivations and gratifications. This suggests that overeducation could promote industrial conflict. Workers with unfulfilled expectations or those who feel their skills are underutilized may become frustrated and cynical about their jobs, resulting in adverse behavior in the workplace. Moreover, overeducation could lead to these conditions by promoting job dissatisfaction, which has been shown to relate to at least some of these conditions (turnover and absenteeism). But again, only further research can substantiate these proposed relationships.

SUMMARY AND CONCLUSION

Because of the lack of direct empirical tests, the preceding review of existing research yields only indirect evidence supporting the view that overeducation may promote poor health, ineffective performance, or adverse workplace behavior. There is, however, some direct empirical support for the proposition that overeducation may lead to job dissatisfaction.

A review of the general research on these subjects adds further support to these propositions. Most theories acknowledge an array of factors that interact simultaneously to influence workplace conditions. These factors fall into two categories, characteristics of individuals and characteristics of jobs. The former category includes the personal needs, aspirations, expectations, skills and abilities, and other attributes of the individual. The latter category includes the physical characteristics of one's job—the content (tasks and autonomy), wages, and promotional possibilities—and the social characteristics—one's peers and supervisors. Job characteristics or individual characteristics may exert independent influences on any workplace condition, either directly or indirectly. For example, a job with a high salary may promote job satisfaction. A complete understanding of these conditions can only come from considering the interaction among all the possible factors.[9] For example, it is unlikely that all individuals with equal salaries are equally satisfied. Perhaps some workers attach little importance to pecuniary rewards.

The complex interaction among factors makes it difficult to assess the influence of any one factor. Most often only net effects are observed. Overeducation may have potentially negative effects in the workplace, but these effects could be mediated by other intervening factors. For example, low salaries may promote job dissatisfaction and poor mental health. The latter condition may not materialize if those individuals find fulfillment outside their jobs that compensates for the dissatisfaction they experience in their jobs.

Within this melange of factors, researchers have identified two that may lead to adverse effects in the workplace. Both of them arise from the discrepancy between the characteristics of individuals and the characteristics of their jobs. The first deals with skills. Research indicates that individuals whose skills (assessed either objectively or subjectively) are underutilized in their jobs are more likely to be dissatisfied, have poorer mental health, and exhibit poorer work performance than other individuals. Research also indicates that workers whose expectations are not realized in their jobs are more dissatisfied, have poorer health, and perform their jobs more poorly. Expectations may concern a job's remuneration, autonomy, or tasks. They may be absolute or based on comparisons with one's peers. Although the evidence is hardly overwhelming, these two factors have repeatedly been identified as having important effects on workplace attitudes and behavior.

These findings lead to some logical inferences about the effects of overeducation. Education generally affects both the characteristics of individuals (their skills and abilities, personality, expectations) as well as the characteristics of their jobs by helping to determine the jobs for which they qualify. Two definitions of overeducation deal with discrepancies between these two sets of characteristics, one based on skills and one based on expectations. Since these discrepancies have been linked previously to adverse consequences in the workplace, one can infer that overeducation may result in similar consequences.

This may not always be the case. In fact, the influence of education in the workplace is rather paradoxical. Education is generally thought to produce positive attitudes and desirable behavior. Highly educated workers hold higher paying and more-challenging jobs and, as a result, are usually more satisfied, more productive, and exhibit better behavior than less-educated workers. Yet overeducation may lead to opposite effects. Overeducated workers may be more dissatisfied than other workers, although they may exhibit good mental health because their education has also given them other avenues of self-fulfillment. The issue of how much these other avenues can compensate for unfulfilling work experiences remains unexplored.

What becomes apparent from this discussion is the need for more research to test these conjectures directly. Nonetheless, negative consequences from overeducation do appear probable from a review of the existing literature.

NOTES

1. For example, see U.S. News and World Report, November 27, 1972; Guzzardi, Jr. 1976; O'Toole 1975a, 1975b; Business Week, February 20, 1978; and Shaffer 1976.

2. It is interesting to note that the aspirations of high school seniors toward professional employment changed very little in the two and one-half years after graduation, despite the poor labor market that existed at the time. See Table 1.

3. These two studies are not exactly comparable since they examine different years, although there is some overlap. The time of the first study falls largely in the prosperous 1960s, while the second deals mainly with the less prosperous period of the early 1970s.

4. Because of the volume of this literature, the discussion draws predominantly on reports that summarize the findings on particular topics. This review also cites those individual studies that test these relationships directly.

5. Marx believed that work could serve as a means of fulfilling personal needs, but, under capitalism, work is degraded in such a way as to lose its capacity for satisfying intrinsic needs.

6. See Sutermeister (1976); Katzell et al. (1975); Schwab and Cummings (1970); Brayfield and Crockett (1955); and Lawler and Porter (1967).

7. Thompson and Borglum (1973) attempt to establish the relationship between negative work attitudes and strike activity, but little can be drawn from their study because of the confounding effects of unionization in the firms that they studied.

8. See Brayfield and Crockett (1955); Vroom (1964); Porter and Steers (1973); Srivastva et al. (1977); and Andrisani et al. (1977).

9. A case in point is the literature on the effects of automation and functional specialization (Blauner 1964; Shepard 1971; Walker and Guest 1952). Some of this research concludes that increased specialization leads to negative work attitudes while some suggests that it leads to positive work attitudes (see discussion in Shepard 1970). Such ambiguous results undoubtedly arise from the differing methodologies employed in these studies. One cannot generalize about the effects of the fragmentation of job tasks without accounting for the characteristics of individuals in those jobs. We would not expect all individuals to react similarly to similar conditions because of differences in their needs, desires, and skills. Only by simultaneously taking account of both job facets and worker differences can one hope to understand what will result in the workplace from changes in jobs or individuals.

6

IMPLICATIONS OF OVEREDUCATION
FOR PUBLIC AND PRIVATE POLICY

Evidence presented in the empirical portion of this study sug-
sts that overeducation is a widespread condition in the contemporary
or market. Overeducation was defined as the discrepancy between
e educational attainments of workers and the educational require-
ents of their jobs. In spite of the limitations of this approach, it is
rd to escape the conclusion that overeducation is a common phenom-
on. Future projections of employment and educational attainments
so indicate that this condition will remain for some time to come.
ese findings do not rule out the possibility that overeducation also
ists according to the other definitions that were outlined in Chapter 1.
e existence of overeducation, no matter how it is measured, may
ompt reforms and policies within both the public and private sectors.
his chapter speculates on the form these responses may take as well
the likelihood that they will occur.

Some people feel that overeducation should be treated as an in-
vidual concern. They see education primarily as a private invest-
ent decision with personal benefits. If individuals are not finding
bs commensurate with their level of skill and training, then perhaps
vestment in education will decline in the future. Individuals who are
onsidering participation in postsecondary schooling must realize
at such an investment may not reap rewards in the labor market, al-
ough there may be other benefits from such an undertaking.

Yet education is more than an individual investment yielding in-
ividual benefits. As the preceding chapter illustrates, overeducation
ould lead to adverse consequences in the workplace. In some in-
tances these responses may simply affect individual welfare by pro-
oting job dissatisfaction. However, any negative effects of overedu-
ation may ultimately affect job performance. When this happens the

117

firms employing such workers may experience threats to product quality and declines in productivity. Firms must take an interest in the welfare of their workers because it also affects the welfare of the firm, particularly its profitability. The case of the Chevrolet Vega assembly plant in Lordstown, Ohio, illustrates this point. At least some of the problems that arose in 1972 at that plant have been attributed to the employment of large numbers of educated workers who rebelled against the production techniques employed there (Aronowitz 1973). Such occurrences point out the need for company policies that deal with the integration of educated workers into the corporate hierarchy.

Education is also more than a private concern. Federal, state, and local governments invest vast social resources in the educational system. At least some of this investment is supposed to yield an adequate return, based on the higher wages and tax payments of more educated workers. Yet, even if relative earnings remain high, the social return to investment in schooling may be declining, as the discussion in Chapter 2 pointed out. The adverse consequences of overeducation in the workplace constitute a social concern as well. Declining productivity and falling profits affect the overall welfare of the economy and the prosperity of the entire country.

Because overeducation constitutes a problem for employers in the private sector and the public at large, public and private policy responses are warranted. But what form will these responses take? To answer this question, it is important to distinguish between what responses are possible and what responses are probable. The former constitute an objective list of alternatives, while the latter also depend on one's view of social change. Recall that the alternative theories of the labor market discussed in Chapter 2 explain the existence of overeducation in different ways. These theories also suggest different private and public policy responses to a condition of overeducation. Consider, for example, the differences between two polar views, a neoclassical and a Marxist perspective.

In a neoclassical perspective one views overeducation in terms of costs and benefits: costs of investment in schooling and the returns to that investment based primarily on earnings. Overeducation based on the underutilization of skills is inconsistent with this view because firms would always make use of the added skills (human capital) of their workers, while worker expectations are beyond this purview. Since overeducation in this conception is simply a short-term cyclical phenomenon, little private or public response is warranted. A decline in the rate-of-return to schooling will result in a decrease in enrollments and a fall in the supply of college graduates entering the labor market. But eventually the rate-of-return will rise owing to the restriction of supply relative to demand. The only response by government should be to ensure that the market operates effectively by providing accurate information for individual investors about the potential outcomes from investment and by ensuring the unrestricted forces of competition on prices (for example, guarding against price fixing or unfair monopolistic policies). Some (Friedman 1962) argue further that government subsidies for education should be eliminated so that students base their decisions on the true costs of investment.

In a Marxist perspective, overeducation can be considered from all respects (earnings, expectations, and the utilization of skills) because, in this view, workers seek more than just adequate salaries from their jobs. Marx believed that work is capable of fulfilling man's fundamental needs for self-esteem and moral purpose as well as providing a means of livelihood (Ollman 1971). The utilization of man's capabilities, including cognitive skills, becomes especially important in this view. One basic contention in a Marxist perspective is that work is degraded in a capitalist economy; tasks are routinized and simplified as a result of capitalists' desires for profits and accumulation (Braverman 1974). Policy responses, both in the private and public sector, must be viewed as a result of class struggles between capitalists and workers whose interests are fundamentally opposed.

As these two perspectives illustrate, each view of the labor market offers different explanations of overeducation and suggests different responses to deal with the condition. In the discussion that follows, I first describe a series of policies and responses that could arise to address the problems of overeducation. I also discuss what responses are likely to occur and what role various groups (employers, unions, and workers) could play in promoting these reforms. The discussion focuses on the private sector first and the public sector second. In the final section, I offer some concluding comments on this study and on the significance of overeducation.

PRIVATE SECTOR

Responses to overeducation in the private sector could take many forms. Some may address the situations of particular overeducated individuals, others may affect a number of individuals through reforms in a firm's salary or promotional policies. Some may involve only cosmetic changes to the physical environment; others may be more substantive, involving changes in decision-making processes. Changes in the utilization of educational skills in the workplace could reduce the incidence of overeducation by making jobs more commensurate with the skills of workers. Other changes could reduce overeducation by making jobs more desirable, thus helping them to conform to workers' expectations.

Changes can be classified into two types, technical and political.[1] Technical changes affect the characteristics of jobs, such as job tasks or the working environment. They could be instituted on a small scale, affecting only particular jobs, or on a large scale, affecting the characteristics of all jobs in a firm. Political changes affect the decision-making processes. Again, they could be adopted at particular places in an organization, or they could affect the overall organization. Technical changes are the easiest to implement because they require little change in the organizational structure. Political changes are more difficult to implement, however, because they involve more fundamental changes in the way work is organized.

The redesign of job tasks offers one of the most promising technical changes (Davis and Taylor 1972; Pierce and Dunham 1976). Essentially this change involves expanding the number of tasks performed in a job, commonly referred to as job enlargement. The same result comes from job rotation, where workers rotate or share jobs, thus increasing the number of tasks performed by each worker. Job redesign can take place at any given level in the job hierarchy, from production jobs to middle-level management positions.

Expanding job tasks could reduce overeducation by utilizing a wider range of the skills that workers possess. It could also help to satisfy workers' expectations about the content of their jobs. As a result, job redesign could also help to redress some of the adverse consequences of overeducation, particularly job dissatisfaction and low productivity. Experiments in job redesign demonstrate marked improvements in job satisfaction and productivity (Katzell et al 1975; Katzell, Bienstock, and Faerstein 1977).

Other technical changes, either at particular places in a firm or instigated on a companywide basis, could also redress the problems of overeducated workers. Promotional policies could be changed to alter workers' expectations concerning advancement opportunities. For example, some companies are developing lateral transfer programs that, in effect, lengthen the time required to achieve vertical promotions (Zonana 1975). Employees' demands or expectations about salaries might be buttressed with profit-sharing plans or other forms of work-incentive plans. Introducing flexible work schedules could help satisfy, albeit in a limited way, workers' desires for autonomy and independence in their jobs. Changes in the physical environment or social organization might also make jobs more appealing, thus helping to satisfy workers' expectations.

More fundamental changes in work involve decision-making processes. A number of innovations could be instituted in existing firms: job enrichment, where the expansion of job tasks includes responsibility for planning and execution as well as for performing; autonomous work groups, where groups of workers are involved in the planning and execution of their jobs; workers' councils, where representatives of workers meet with management and help make decisions about how the company is run; and employee representation on corporate boards, where workers' representatives are involved in decision making at the highest level of management. Changes of this type involve various degrees of participatory management, where workers take on some of the decision-making responsibilities traditionally held by managers. A consequence of these changes is often a flattening of the job hierarchy since some levels of management may be subsumed in other jobs.

Political changes of the type just described could help redress the problem of overeducation by making more use of workers' skills. In particular, participatory management would require reasoning and communication skills of all workers, not simply managers. These changes could also reduce overeducation by making work more interesting and challenging, thus bringing workers' jobs more in line with their expectations. Examples of these types of political changes can be found in Europe (Jenkins 1973). Although these innovations are less common domestically, most experiments indicate that they hold promise for redressing the problems that could result from overeducation, particularly high turnover, job dissatisfaction, and low productivity (Katzell, Bienstock, and Faerstein 1977; Rosenberg and Rosenstein 1980; U.S., Department of Health, Education and Welfare 1973, chap. 4).

The most radical change in the structure of work involves complete employee ownership and control—industrial democracy. In the political changes described above, workers become involved in various levels of decision making, but the ultimate authority still resides with the owners of the firms, who also receive the profits. In employee-owned and -managed firms, commonly referred to as cooperatives, workers not only participate in all the decision making, but they also receive the profits that the company realizes as a result of their efforts. In cooperatives, collective incentives replace individual incentives. Thus, absenteeism, turnover, and other forms of adverse work behavior occur less frequently than in capitalist firms (Levin 1980b; Carnoy and Shearer 1980). Furthermore, because these firms are managed democratically, work can be organized for the collective benefit of the employees. As a result, overeducation—at least underutilization of skills—is unlikely to exist in such a setting.

Cooperatives are also able to rotate work roles among members and train workers for a variety of jobs. This convention enhances the attachment and interest of workers in the work process and organization relative to performing a routine and repetitive task, and it also improves their ability to work with colleagues in a flexible manner.

> Likewise, it gives them an opportunity for continuous skill development and reduces the problem of absenteeism of any particular worker on any particular day, since several workers can perform any particular task. [Levin 1980b, p. 27]

In fact, cooperatives offer the potential to fully utilize all workers' skills, capacities, and talents—what Maslow (1970) calls self-actualization.

> In the workplace, self-actualization requires the freedom of workers to assert their individuality and to control their activities both individually and collectively. It requires the development of work as an intrinsically satisfying human endeavor in which the ability of persons to mold the work process exceeds the ability of the work process to mold the personalities and activities of the persons carrying out the work tasks. It requires that workers benefit from the products of their own labor and determine collectively what they will produce and how they will produce it. In short, it requires the ability to utilize one's human attributes in productive ways to influence and shape the productive process, and to derive healthy social relationships with one's co-workers in governing democratically the work organization. [Levin 1980b, pp. 29-30]

Evaluations of existing cooperatives, although few, support these claims (Levin 1980b; Jenkins 1973; Frieden 1980).

The technical and political changes just described constitute a variety of reforms and possible solutions to the problem of overeducation in the workplace. Some of the changes, such as job enlargement, can be instituted rather easily within the existing organizational structure of most capitalist firms. Others, such as the creation of cooperatives, involve radical changes in both the organizational structure and the technical nature of jobs. Technical changes are more easily implemented and hence more likely to be adopted; conversely, political changes are less likely to be adopted. But workers, employers, and unions may also play a role in determining which workplace reforms are likely to be adopted.

Since employers have almost complete control over the production process in the capitalist economy that exists in this country, they are most likely to initiate the reforms in the workplace that will address their problems. The reforms they are most likely to adopt are the ones that involve the fewest fundamental changes in the decision prerogatives of management—that is, technical changes, such as job redesign or job rotation. Employers are less likely to adopt reforms or policies that alter their decision prerogatives or threaten their control over the work structure (political changes that give workers decision-making capacities). Workers in this country have little real power in determining the structure of work (Marglin 1974; Braverman 1974; Behn 1974). Although workers may force employers to take action as a result of their adverse workplace activity, they will have little voice in the structure that these reforms will take.

Changes are most likely to arise in those firms that are plagued financially by labor problems. A variety of reforms and policies have been adopted by particular plants of a company, or an entire company, in order to maintain or enhance profitability (Walton 1974). If the incidence of overeducation continues to grow as estimates suggest, the number of companies adopting these policies will grow accordingly. But reforms will not appear quickly. Companies may initially resist adopting any meaningful reform policies. The policies that are adopted will always depend on other forces that may influence workplace conditions, especially the state of the external labor market. In periods of high unemployment, reforms to counteract potentially disruptive workplace conditions may be unnecessary since the labor force can be disciplined with the threat of dismissal. In a tight external labor market, however, threats of dismissal may have little effect and reform policies may be the only alternative.

What role will unions play in this process? Unions could play an active role in the decision-making processes of companies, as they do in many Western European countries (Sturmthal 1977). In the United States, however, unions have traditionally played a limited role in decision making. Their bargaining rights with employers are largely confined to salaries, benefits, and policies regarding promotions and dismissals (Behn 1974). Unions have little to do with how work is organized and structured within the firm. Consequently, they are unlikely to institute any workplace reforms in response to overeducation. Some critics even charge that union officials promote the interests of capitalist employers at the expense of the welfare of the rank and file (Aronowitz 1973).

Workers themselves are also unlikely to play an active role in adopting workplace reforms. They have limited opportunities within the structure of most capitalist firms. In some instances, workers have bought and taken control of firms that their capitalist owners deemed unprofitable (Jenkins 1973). But such instances are rare. Presently there are a variety of obstacles to the widespread expansion of cooperatives in this country including legal difficulties, limited access to requisite capital, and training opportunities necessary for successful self-management (Levin 1980b). Thus, without fundamental changes in the capitalist-oriented society, widespread adoption of worker-initiated reforms is unlikely.

In summary, the response to overeducation in the private sector will largely come from firms that experience problems of declining productivity, high turnover, and other forms of adverse workplace behavior associated with overeducation. Technical changes in the nature of particular jobs are more likely to be adopted than political changes that involve sharing decision making within the firm. Unions and workers will play a limited role in instituting work reforms and will only do so as a result of more fundamental changes in the capitalist structure of the present economy.

PUBLIC POLICY

Should public policy be concerned with overeducation? Although the ill effects of overeducation are most likely to be felt within the private sector, such adverse effects may be felt outside of the firms themselves. The government has long been concerned with the public's welfare as well as with a healthy business environment. More important, however, is the great public investment in the educational system, an investment that exceeded $140 billion in 1977 (Grant and Lind 1979, p. 27). Because of overeducation, the government's investment may be yielding a poor return.

Government policy could focus on two areas: the utilization of educated workers within the private and public sectors (demand) or the number and distribution of educated workers entering the labor market (supply). Government policy cannot address itself to the structure of the work process found in the private sector. Only certain basic rights (such as freedom from unnecessary health hazards) fall within the province of government regulation. It would be difficult to make a case for government intervention on behalf of under-utilized, educated workers who may exhibit overt signs of job dissatisfaction or poor work performance. First, evidence on causality is both weak and insufficient. Second, it is the fundamental right of employers to have full control over the utilization of labor and the form of production within our capitalist economy (Behn 1974).

Nevertheless, the government can affect the demand for labor within the private sector through macroeconomic policies. The government could provide tax incentives for firms to make better use of skilled workers. Interest rates, which affect the ability of companies to borrow money for capital expenditures, are influenced by government monetary policies. The government could retard the replacement of skilled labor by capital through policies that would act to raise the interest rates. The government could also take more direct action to deal with the utilization of educated workers in the private sector. If productivity declines in certain industries, in part, because of an overeducated work force, the government could provide seed money for firms to experiment on reorganizing work processes so that the educational skills of workers are better utilized. The government could also provide funds for companies that are interested in promoting changes in the relationship between employers and employees that would give workers more decision-making power. More specifically, the government could encourage the growth of employee-owned and -managed firms through tax incentives and by providing subsidized loans.

In general, government policy is unlikely to affect substantially the problem of overeducation in the private sector. Government policies are most often formulated by economists who ascribe to a neo-classical view of the labor market, a view that advocates minimal government interference in the private sector. Liberal influences, however, will force the government into taking some action to address the problems arising from overeducation. Radicals, who see the underlying cause of overeducation rooted in the dominant class position of capitalists in the economy, would argue that overeducation is unlikely to disappear as long as the fundamental characteristics of capitalism remain unaltered.

The government can affect the overall demand for labor through policies that affect its own work force. Public sector employment has grown continuously during the last 30 years, reaching a point where one-sixth of the employed population worked in some level of government (federal, state, or local) by 1978 (U.S., Bureau of Labor Statistics 1979a, p. 264). The public sector also employs a higher percentage of college-educated male workers than the private sector. Almost one-half (49.4 percent) of all males employed in government in 1978, for example, had completed at least one year of college, compared with only one-third (37.0 percent) of male workers generally (U.S., Bureau of Labor Statistics 1979a, p. A-21). Thus, the public sector could help alleviate the oversupply of college graduates by increasing the size of its work force. As the demand for government services continues to grow in the future, public sector employment could grow accordingly. But there are constraints to growth as well. O'Connor (1973) argues that the government has taken on too many functions over the years in an effort to provide a suitable climate for capitalistic expansion. This action has resulted in growing fiscal problems within the government. There has also been growing concern by taxpayers about the escalating increases in taxes, particularly property taxes (Time, June 5, 1978). Any future reform of the tax system could result in decreased government budgets that would curtail the growth of government employment.

Public policy is also capable of affecting the educational attainments of workers entering the labor force by changing the private costs of education. Some critics (Friedman 1962) have repeatedly argued for little, if any, public investment in education, particularly at the postsecondary level. The argument is based on the premise that education is basically a private investment involving private costs (tuition and forgone earnings) and yielding private benefits (increased earnings and nonpecuniary returns). If the public also benefits from such an investment, then so much the better; but such "spillover" effects do not require or justify public investment. So the story goes. A more liberal view, predominant in our country, holds public investment in education to be necessary and desirable (Bowen et al. 1977). For instance, large public subsidies for postsecondary education in the late 1950s were justified by the need for more university-trained scientists and engineers to join the space race.

Currently, the heavy subsidization of education, at least at the federal level, is ostensibly justified on the grounds of equity. Many people believe that schooling promotes social mobility by ensuring fairness in the race for life's unequal economic rewards. Children from disadvantaged backgrounds receive compensatory education and students from low-income families receive subsidies for postsecondary schooling. It is unclear whether government subsidies really achieve their intended purpose, but funds are secured continuously for these programs under the pretense that they promote social mobility.

The question remains, Can public policy do anything about the condition of overeducation? Although it may seem easy for the government to reduce its subsidy of postsecondary education in order to diminish an oversupply of college graduates entering the labor market, the political consequences are formidable. Such action may be socially efficient, but it will affect equity as well. A curtailing of public funds would have to be done in such a manner as not to impair the present or desired equity of such funding.

Of course, to say such action is possible does not mean that it is politically feasible. In general, it is difficult for the government to reduce the amount of its funding. Perhaps its future growth could be curtailed. But even that move may not be feasible politically. There is already pressure on the federal government to increase its postsecondary education subsidies to middle-income families (Longanecker 1980). So government policy regarding the funding of education may do little to alleviate the condition of overeducation.

Other government action is possible. The government may be able to alter the content and form of the education it subsidizes. It can satisfy the pressures for more postsecondary schooling by promoting the community college systems. Some critics (Karabel 1972; Bowles and Gintis 1976) argue that the rapid growth of the community colleges in the last decade was the means of satisfying the demand for

more postsecondary schooling without jeapordizing the role of tradi-
tional four-year colleges in preparing individuals for the highest levels of the job hierarchy. Moreover, the recurring movement of career
education may be a way of getting students interested in jobs with specific skills that predominate at the middle levels of the job hierarchy,
thus lessening the demand for higher levels of schooling and higher-
status jobs (Grubb and Lazerson 1975). The government could also
promote the idea of recurrent education (participation in postsecondary
schooling at different stages in workers' careers) as a means of reducing the demand for schooling immediately after high school. But
employment patterns reveal that those with less schooling have more
difficulty in finding employment than those with a college education
(Golladay 1977, p. 123). Thus, individuals seeking social mobility
are unlikely to forgo participation in postsecondary schooling.

   In summary, it seems that government policy can do little more
than promote the public's interest in particular levels or types of
schooling. These actions may have some effect on the burgeoning
numbers of overeducated workers, but they are unlikely to stem the
increasing tide of overeducated workers in the long run. As long as
education is seen as a means of achieving social mobility, the interest
and the incentive to obtain more education will continue. The condition of overeducation, therefore, will probably remain.

CONCLUSION

   The tone of this chapter may appear unduly pessimistic. Perhaps it is. But a condition of overeducation appears to have existed
for some time now, and it appears that it will continue for some time
in the future. Others have expressed concern previously about the
growing numbers of educated workers entering the labor force, particularly those with postsecondary schooling (Harris 1949; Berg 1970;
Rawlins and Ulman 1974). More will undoubtedly do so in the future.
On the other hand, defenders of the present schooling system (Carnegie Commission 1973) always counter such pessimism with the many
virtues of postsecondary schooling that accrue outside of the labor
market.

   The overall conclusion of this study can be stated quite suc-
cinctly. As long as those with more schooling fare better in the labor
market than those with less schooling, overeducation will continue to
exist. Public support of education will remain. The private sector
will change the structure of work only to the extent that is necessary
to maintain profitability. Individuals will continue to compete for the
few really good jobs in the economy, blaming only themselves if they
fail to acquire them. This is not to say, however, that no change will

take place, but only that such changes will leave unaltered the fundamental structures and conditions in our society.

How one views overeducation—whether or not one believes it exists, for what reasons, and what will happen in the future—ultimately depends upon one's view of the world. Some believe that overeducation is a condition affecting certain individuals within the labor market, a condition perpetuated by individuals making misinformed investment decisions (Freeman 1976). In this view, such market anomalies inevitably arise from time to time in a market-regulated economy and will always resolve themselves through the same market system.

Others believe that as long as we maintain and support the type of society in which we presently live—with its large hierarchical and bureaucratized organizations and with the predominantly private ownership of the means of production—little will happen to alleviate this condition. In fact, they argue that a capitalist form of production necessarily causes a subjugation and degradation of human labor (Marx 1967; Braverman 1974; Bowles and Gintis 1976; Levin et al. forthcoming). Furthermore, only by making fundamental changes can our capitalist society move toward a democratic socialist state, as Marx believed.

Differences between these two views will remain unresolved by any objective social science evidence.

NOTE

1. Levin (1976) and Behn (1974) provide a more detailed taxonomy of workplace reforms.

BIBLIOGRAPHY

Andrisani, Paul J., et al. 1977. Work Attitudes and Labor Market Experience: Evidence from the National Longitudinal Surveys. Philadelphia: Center for Labor and Human Resource Studies.

Aronowitz, Stanley. 1973. False Promises: The Shaping of American Working Class Consciousness. New York: McGraw-Hill.

Baran, Paul A. 1957. The Political Economy of Growth. New York: Monthly Review Press.

Beck, E. M., Patrick M. Horan, and Charles M. Tolbert II. 1978. "Stratification in a Dual Economy: A Sectoral Model of Earnings Determination." American Sociological Review 43 (October): 704-20.

Becker, Gary S. 1975. Human Capital. 2d ed. New York: National Bureau of Economic Research.

Behn, William H. 1974. "Classification of Work Organizations." Mimeographed. Menlo Park, Calif.: Portola Institute.

Ben-Porath, Yoram. 1967. "The Production of Human Capital and the Life Cycle of Earnings." Journal of Political Economy 75 (August): 352-65.

Berg, Ivar. 1970. Education and Jobs: The Great Training Robbery. New York: Praeger.

Berg, Ivar, Marcia Freedman, and Michael Freeman. 1978. Managers and Work Reform: A Limited Engagement. New York: Free Press.

Bielby, William T., and Arne L. Kalleberg. 1975. "The Differentiation of Occupations." Discussion Paper. Mimeographed. Madison: Institute for Research on Poverty, University of Wisconsin-Madison.

Bird, Caroline. 1975. The Case against College. New York: David McKay.

Bisconti, Ann S., and Lewis C. Solmon. 1977. Job Satisfaction after College: The Graduates' Viewpoint. Bethlehem, Pa.: CPC Foundation.

_____. 1976. College Education on the Job: The Graduates' Viewpoint. Bethlehem, Pa.: CPC Foundation.

Blau, Peter M., and Otis Dudley Duncan. 1967. The American Occupational Structure. New York: John Wiley & Sons.

Blaug, Mark. 1970. An Introduction to the Economics of Education. Baltimore: Penguin Books.

Blauner, Robert. 1964. Alienation and Freedom. Chicago: University of Chicago Press.

Bowen, Howard R., et al. 1977. Investment in Learning: The Individual and Social Value of American Higher Education. San Francisco: Jossey-Bass.

Bowles, Samuel, and Herbert Gintis. 1976. Schooling in Capitalist America. New York: Basic Books.

Bowman, Mary Jean. 1964. "Schultz, Denison, and the Contribution of 'EDS' to National Income Growth." Journal of Political Economy 72 (October): 450-64.

Braverman, Harry. 1974. Labor and Monopoly Capital: The Degradation of Work in the Twentieth Century. New York: Monthly Review Press.

Brayfield, Arthur H., and Walter H. Crockett. 1955. "Employee Attitudes and Employee Performance." Psychological Bulletin 52 (September): 396-424.

Business Week. 1978. February 20, pp. 64-70.

Cain, Glen C. 1976. "The Challenge of Segmented Labor Market Theories to Orthodox Theory: A Survey." Journal of Economic Literature 14 (December): 1215-57.

Carnegie Commission on Higher Education. 1973. College Graduates and Jobs: Adjusting to a New Labor Market Situation. New York: McGraw-Hill.

Carnoy, Martin. 1980. "Segmented Labour Markets." In Education, Work, and Employment, edited by Martin Carnoy, Henry M. Levin, and Kenneth King, vol. 2, pp. 9-121. Paris: United Nations Educational, Scientific and Cultural Organization, International Institute for Educational Planning.

Carnoy, Martin, and Derek Shearer. 1980. Economic Democracy. White Plains, N.Y.: Sharp.

Carter, Michael, and Martin Carnoy. 1974. "Theories of Labor Markets and Worker Productivity." Discussion Paper 74-4. Mimeographed. Palo Alto, Calif.: Center for Economic Studies, August.

Chiswick, Barry R. 1973. "Schooling, Screening, and Income." In Does College Matter? edited by Lewis C. Solmon and Paul J. Taubman, pp. 151-58. New York: Academic Press.

Coburn, David. 1975. "Job-Worker Incongruence: Consequences for Health." Journal of Health and Social Behavior 16 (June): 198-212.

Cohn, Elchanan. 1975. The Economics of Education. Cambridge, Mass.: Ballinger.

D'Amico, Ronald J. 1978. "Earnings Attainment and Job Hierarchies in Monopoly and Competitive Capital Sectors." Ph.D. dissertation, Johns Hopkins University.

Davis, Louis E., and James C. Taylor, eds. 1972. Design of Jobs. Baltimore: Penguin Books.

Denison, Edward F. 1971. "Measuring the Contribution of Education (and the 'Residual') to Economic Growth." In Readings in the Economics of Education, edited by Mary Jean Bowman et al., pp. 315-37. Paris: United Nations Educational, Scientific and Cultural Organization.

Diamond, Daniel E., and Hrach Bedrosian. 1970. "Hiring Standards and Job Performance." U.S. Department of Labor, Manpower Research Monograph No. 18. Washington, D.C.: Government Printing Office.

Doeringer, Peter B., and Michael J. Piore. 1971. Internal Labor Markets and Manpower Analysis. Lexington, Mass.: Heath Lexington Books.

Duncan, Greg J. 1976. "Earnings Functions and Nonpecuniary Benefits." Journal of Human Resources 11 (Fall): 462-83.

Eckaus, R. S. 1964. "Economic Criteria for Education and Training." Review of Economics and Statistics 46 (May): 181-90.

Edwards, Richard. 1979. Contested Terrain. New York: Basic Books.

Fine, Sidney A. 1968. "The Use of the Dictionary of Occupational Titles as a Source of Estimates of Educational and Training Requirements." Journal of Human Resources 3 (Summer): 363-75.

Flanagan, R. , G. Strauss, and L. Ulman. 1974. "Worker Discontent and Work Place Behavior." Reprint no. 388. Berkeley, Calif.: University of California, Institute of Industrial Relations.

Freedman, Marcia K. , and Gretchen Maclachlan. 1976. Labor Markets: Segments and Shelters. Montclair, N.J.: Allanheld, Osmun.

Freeman, Richard B. 1979. "The Effect of Demographic Factors on Age-Earnings Profiles." Journal of Human Resources 14 (Summer): 289-318.

_____. 1977. "The Decline in the Economic Rewards to College Education." Review of Economics and Statistics 59 (February): 18-29.

_____. 1976. The Overeducated American. New York: Academic Press.

_____. 1975. "Overinvestment in College Training?" Journal of Human Resources 10 (Summer): 287-311.

_____. 1971. The Market for College-Trained Manpower: A Study in the Economics of Career Choice. Cambridge, Mass.: Harvard University Press.

Frieden, Karl. 1980. "Workplace Democracy and Productivity." Washington, D.C.: National Center for Economic Alternatives.

Friedman, Milton. 1962. Capitalism and Freedom. Chicago: University of Chicago Press.

Gardell, Bertil. 1976. "Technology, Alienation and Mental Health: Summary of a Social Psychological Study of Technology and the Worker." Acta Sociologica 19: 83-93.

Golladay, Mary A. 1977. The Condition of Education, 1977 Edition. Washington, D. C.: U. S. Government Printing Office.

_____. 1976. The Condition of Education, 1976 Edition. Washington, D. C.: U. S. Government Printing Office.

Goodman, Ellen. 1980. "BAMAMA." Washington Post, May 29, p. A19.

Gordon, David M. 1972. Theories of Poverty and Underemployment: Orthodox, Radical, and Dual Labor Market Perspectives. Lexington, Mass.: D. C. Heath.

Gordon, Margaret S. 1974. "The Changing Labor Market for College Graduates." In Higher Education and the Labor Market, edited by Margaret S. Gordon, pp. 27-81. New York: McGraw-Hill.

Grant, W. Vance, and C. George Lind. 1979. Digest of Education Statistics 1979. Washington, D. C.: U. S. Government Printing Office.

Grasso, John T. 1977. "On the Declining Labor Market Value of Schooling." Paper prepared for the 1977 Annual Meeting of the American Educational Research Association, New York City, April 4-8.

Griliches, Zvi. 1977. "Estimating the Returns to Schooling: Some Econometric Problems." Econometrica 45 (January): 1-22.

_____. 1969. "Capital-Skill Complementarity." Review of Economics and Statistics 51 (November): 465-68.

Grubb, W. Norton, and Marvin Lazerson. 1975. "Rally 'Round the Workplace: Continuities and Fallacies in Career Education." Harvard Educational Review 45 (November): 451-74.

Guzzardi, Walter, Jr. 1976. "The Uncertain Passage from College to Job." Fortune 93 (January): 126-29.

Harris, Seymour E. 1949. The Market for College Graduates. Cambridge, Mass.: Harvard University Press.

Harrison, Bennett. 1972. Education, Training, and the Urban Ghetto. Baltimore: Johns Hopkins University Press.

Herzberg, F., B. Mausner, and B. Snyderman. 1959. The Motivation to Work. 2d ed. New York: John Wiley & Sons.

House, James S. 1974. "The Effects of Occupational Stress on Physical Health." In Work and the Quality of Life, edited by James O'Toole, pp. 145-70. Cambridge, Mass.: MIT Press.

Jenkins, David. 1973. Job Power: Blue and White Collar Democracy. Baltimore: Penguin Books.

Johnson, George E. 1970. "The Demand for Labor by Educational Category." Southern Economic Journal 37 (October): 190-204.

Kalleberg, Arne L. 1977. "Work Values and Job Rewards: A Theory of Job Satisfaction." American Sociological Review 42 (February): 124-43.

Kalleberg, Arne L., and Aage B. Sorensen. 1973. "The Measurement of the Effects of Overtraining on Job Attitudes." Sociological Methods and Research 2 (November): 215-38.

Karabel, Jerome. 1972. "Community Colleges and Social Stratification." Harvard Educational Review 42 (November): 521-62.

Kasl, Stanislav V. 1974. "Work and Mental Health." In Work and the Quality of Life, edited by James O'Toole, pp. 171-96. Cambridge, Mass.: MIT Press.

Katz, Daniel. 1954. "Satisfactions and Deprivations in Industrial Life." In Industrial Conflict, edited by Arthur Kornhauser, Robert Dubin, and Arthur M. Ross, pp. 86-106. New York: McGraw-Hill.

Katzell, Raymond A., et al. 1975. Work, Productivity, and Job Satisfaction. New York: New York University Press.

Katzell, Raymond A., Penny Bienstock, and Paul H. Faerstein. 1977. A Guide to Worker Productivity Experiments in the United States 1971-75. New York: New York University Press.

Kolstad, Andrew J. 1976. "Sources of Occupational Prestige: A Study of Public Opinion." Ph.D. dissertation, Stanford University.

Kornhauser, Arthur. 1965. Mental Health of the Industrial Worker. New York: John Wiley & Sons.

Lawler, Edward E., III, and Lyman W. Porter. 1967. "The Effects of Performance on Job Satisfaction." Industrial Relations 7 (October): 20-28.

Levin, Henry M. 1980a. "Workplace Democracy and Educational Planning." In Education, Work, and Employment, edited by Martin Carnoy, Henry M. Levin, and Kenneth King, vol. 2, pp. 123-216. Paris: United Nations Educational, Scientific and Cultural Organization, International Institute for Educational Planning.

_____. 1980b. "Improving the Creative Potential of Human Resources with Producer Cooperatives: Employment, Productivity, and Self-Actualization." Invited Paper for the Sixth World Congress of the International Economic Association, Mexico City, August 4-8.

_____. 1976. "A Taxonomy of Educational Reforms for Changes in the Nature of Work." In The Limits of Educational Reform, edited by Martin Carnoy and Henry M. Levin, pp. 83-114. New York: David McKay.

Levin, Henry M., et al. Forthcoming. The Dialectic of Education and Work. Stanford, Calif.: Stanford University Press.

Longanecker, David. 1980. "Federal Student Assistance: Issues and Option." Budget Issue Paper of the Congressional Budget Office. Washington, D.C.: U.S. Government Printing Office.

Lucas, Robert E. B. 1977. "Hedonic Wage Equations and Psychic Wages in the Returns to Schooling." American Economic Review 67 (September): 549-58.

_____. 1972. "Working Conditions, Wage Rates and Human Capital: A Hedonic Study." Ph.D. dissertation, Massachusetts Institute of Technology.

Mangione, Thomas W., and Robert P. Quinn. 1975. "Job Satisfaction, Counterproductive Behavior, and Drug Use at Work." Journal of Applied Psychology 60 (February): 114–16.

Marglin, Stephen A. 1974. "What Do Bosses Do?" Review of Radical Political Economics 6 (Summer): 60–112.

Margolis, Bruce L., and William H. Kroes. 1974. "Work and the Health of Man." In Work and the Quality of Life, edited by James O'Toole, pp. 133–44. Cambridge, Mass.: MIT Press.

Marx, Karl. 1967. Capital. 3 vols. Translated from the third German edition by Samuel Moore and Edward Aveling, edited by Frederick Engels. New York: International.

Maslow, Abraham H. 1970. Motivation and Personality. 2d ed. New York: Harper & Row.

Miller, Ann R. 1971. "Occupations of the Labor Force according to the Dictionary of Occupational Titles." Mimeographed. Philadelphia: Pennsylvania University, Population Studies Center.

Miller, Ann R., et al., eds. Forthcoming. The Dictionary of Occupational Titles: A Critical Review. Washington, D.C.: National Academy Press.

Mills, C. Wright. 1951. White Collar: The American Middle Classes New York: Oxford University Press.

Mincer, Jacob. 1974. Schooling, Experience, and Earnings. New York: National Bureau of Economic Research.

National Data Use and Access Laboratories. 1973. Technical Documentation for the 1960 Public Use Sample. Rosslyn, Va.: DUALabs.

Nelson, R. R., and E. S. Phelps. 1966. "Investment in Humans, Technological Diffusion, and Economic Growth." American Economic Review 56 (May): 69–75.

Nicholson, Nigel, Colin A. Brown, and J. K. Chadwick-Jones. 1976. "Absence from Work and Job Satisfaction." Journal of Applied Psychology 61 (December): 728–37.

O'Connor, James. 1973. The Fiscal Crisis of the State. New York:
St. Martin's Press.

Oi, Walter Y. 1962. "Labor as a Quasi-Fixed Factor." Journal of
Political Economy 70 (December): 538-55.

Ollman, Bertell. 1971. Alienation: Marx's Conception of Man in
Capitalist Society. Cambridge: At the University Press.

Osterman, Paul. 1975. "An Empirical Study of Labor Market Segmentation." Industrial and Labor Relations Review 28 (July):
508-21.

O'Toole, James. 1975a. "The Reserve Army of the Underemployed:
I—The World of Work." Change 7 (May): 26-33, 63.

_____. 1975b. "The Reserve Army of the Underemployed: II—The
Role of Education." Change 7 (June): 26-33, 60-63.

Pettman, Barrie O., ed. 1975. Labour Turnover and Retention.
Guildford, England: Gower Press.

Pierce, Jon L., and Randall B. Dunham. 1976. "Task Design: A
Literature Review." Academy of Management Science 1 (October): 83-97.

Piore, Michael J. 1975. "Notes on a Theory of Labor Market Segmentation." In Labor Market Segmentation, edited by R. C.
Edwards, M. Reich, and D. M. Gordon, pp. 125-50. Lexington, Mass.: D. C. Heath.

_____. 1973. "Fragments of a 'Sociological' Theory of Wages."
American Economic Review 63 (May): 377-84.

Porter, Lyman W., and Edward E. Lawler, III. 1968. Managerial
Attitudes and Performance. Homewood, Ill.: Richard D. Irwin.

Porter, Lyman W., and Richard M. Steers. 1973. "Organizational,
Work, and Personal Factors in Employee Turnover and Absenteeism." Psychological Bulletin 80 (August): 151-76.

Quinn, Robert P., and Martha S. Mandilovitch. 1975. "Education
and Job Satisfaction: A Questionable Payoff." Ann Arbor,
Mich.: University of Michigan, Survey Research Center, November.

138 / OVEREDUCATION IN THE U.S. LABOR MARKET

Quinn, Robert P., and Linda J. Shepard. 1974. The 1972-73 Quality of Employment Survey: Descriptive Statistics, with Comparison Data from the 1969-70 Survey of Working Conditions. Ann Arbor: University of Michigan, Survey Research Center.

Quinn, Robert P., Graham L. Staines, and Margaret R. McCullough. 1974. Job Satisfaction: Is There a Trend? Manpower Research Monograph no. 30. Washington, D.C.: U.S. Government Printing Office.

Rawlins, V. Lane, and Lloyd Ulman. 1974. "The Utilization of College-Trained Manpower in the United States." In Higher Education and the Labor Market, edited by Margaret S. Gordon, pp. 195-235. New York: McGraw-Hill.

Reich, Michael, David M. Gordon, and Richard C. Edwards. 1973. "A Theory of Labor Market Segmentation." American Economic Review 63 (May): 359-65.

Rosen, Sherwin. 1972. "Learning and Experience in the Labor Market." Journal of Human Resources 7 (Summer): 326-42.

Rosenberg, Richard D., and Eliezer Rosenstein. 1980. "Participation and Productivity: An Empirical Study." Industrial and Labor Relations Review 33 (April): 355-67.

Rumberger, Russell W. Forthcoming. "The Changing Skill Requirements of Jobs in the U.S. Economy." Industrial and Labor Relations Review.

_____. 1980. "The Economic Decline of College Graduates: Fact or Fallacy?" Journal of Human Resources 15 (Winter): 99-112.

Rumberger, Russell W., and Martin Carnoy. 1980. "Segmentation in the U.S. Labour Market: Its Effects on the Mobility and Earnings of Whites and Blacks." Cambridge Journal of Economics 4: 117-32.

Schultz, Theodore W. 1975. "The Value of the Ability to Deal with Disequilibria." Journal of Economic Literature 13 (September): 827-46.

_____. 1961. "Investment in Human Capital." American Economic Review 51 (March): 1-17.

Schwab, Donald P. , and Larry L. Cummings. 1970. "Theories of
Performance and Satisfaction: A Review." Industrial Relations
9 (October): 408-30.

Scoville, James G. 1972. Manpower and Occupational Analysis:
Concepts and Measurement. Lexington, Mass.: D. C. Heath.

_____. 1966. "Education and Training Requirements for Occupa-
tions." Review of Economics and Statistics 48 (November):
387-94.

Sexton, Patricia C. 1977. Women and Work. U.S. Department of
Labor, Research and Development Monograph 46. Washington,
D. C. : Government Printing Office.

Shaffer, Richard A. 1976. "More Americans Take Jobs for Which
They Are Overqualified." Wall Street Journal, January 16, pp.
1, 21.

Sheils, Merrill, et al. 1976. "Who Needs College?" Newsweek,
April 26, pp. 60-69.

Shepard, Jon M. 1971. Automation and Alienation: A Study of Office
and Factory Workers. Cambridge, Mass.: MIT Press.

_____. 1970. "Functional Specialization, Alienation, and Job Satis-
faction." Industrial and Labor Relations Review 23 (January):
207-19.

Sheppard, Harold L. , and Neal Q. Herrick. 1972. Where Have All
the Robots Gone? Worker Dissatisfaction in the '70s. New
York: Free Press.

Slocum, John W. , Jr. 1970. "Performance and Satisfaction: An
Analysis." Industrial Relations 9 (October): 431-36.

Smith, James P. , and Finis Welch. 1978. "Local Labor Markets and
Cyclic Components in Demand for College Trained Manpower."
Annales de l'INSEE 30-31 (April-September): 599-630.

Spence, Michael. 1973. "Job Market Signaling." Quarterly Journal
of Economics 87 (August): 355-74.

Spenner, Kenneth I. 1979. "Temporal Changes in Work Content."
American Sociological Review 44 (December): 968-75.

Srivastva, Suresh, et al. 1977. Job Satisfaction and Productivity. Kent, Ohio: Kent State University, Comparative Administration Research Institute.

Staines, Graham L., and Robert P. Quinn. 1979. "American Workers Evaluate the Quality of Their Jobs." Monthly Labor Review 102 (January): 3-12.

State of California, Employment Development Department. 1976. Occupational Code Conversion System. Mimeographed. Los Angeles: State of California, April.

Sturmthal, Adolf F. 1977. "Unions and Industrial Democracy." Annals of the American Academy of Political and Social Science 431 (May): 12-21.

Sutermeister, Robert A. 1976. People and Productivity. 3d ed. New York: McGraw-Hill.

Taubman, Paul, and Terence Wales. 1975. "Education as an Investment and a Screening Device." In Education, Income, and Human Behavior, edited by F. Thomas Juster, pp. 95-121. New York: McGraw-Hill.

Temme, Lloyd V. 1975. Occupation: Meanings and Measures. Washington, D.C.: Bureau of Social Science Research.

Thompson, Duane E., and Richard P. Borglum. 1973. "A Case Study of Employee Attitudes and Labor Unrest." Industrial and Labor Relations Review 27 (October): 74-83.

Thurow, Lester C. 1975. Generating Inequality: Mechanisms of Distribution in the U.S. Economy. New York: Basic Books.

_____. 1974. "Measuring the Economic Benefits of Education." In Higher Education and the Labor Market, edited by Margaret S. Gordon, pp. 373-418. New York: McGraw-Hill.

_____. 1972. "Education and Economic Equality." Public Interest, no. 28 (Summer), pp. 66-81.

Time. 1978. June 5, pp. 12-14.

_____. 1976. March 29, pp. 46-48.

Trent, James W. 1970. "The Decision to Go to College: An Accumulative Multivariate Process. " In Trends in Postsecondary Education, edited by U.S. , Department of Health, Education and Welfare, Office of Education, pp. 1-30. Washington, D.C.: Government Printing Office.

U.S. , Bureau of Labor Statistics. 1979a. "Educational Attainment of Workers—Some Trends from 1973 to 1978. " Special Labor Force Report 225. Washington, D.C.: Government Printing Office.

_____. 1979b. "Occupational Projections and Training Data. " Bulletin 2020. Washington, D.C.: Government Printing Office.

_____. 1975. Matching Occupational Classifications to Vocational Education Program Codes. Tomorrow's Manpower Needs, Supplement 3 (rev.). Washington, D.C.: Government Printing Office.

_____. 1974a. "Employment of Recent College Graduates, October 1972. " Special Labor Force Report 169. Washington, D.C.: Government Printing Office.

_____. 1974b. "Education of Workers: Projections to 1990. " Special Labor Force Report 160. Washington, D.C.: Government Printing Office.

U.S. , Bureau of the Census. 1978. "An Evaluation of 1970 Census Occupational Classification: The Postcensal Manpower Survey-Census Match Study. " Technical Paper No. 41. Washington, D.C.: Government Printing Office, February.

_____. 1977. "Technical Documentation—Annual Demographic File 1976. " Mimeographed. Washington, D.C.: Bureau of the Census, September.

_____. 1972. Public Use Samples of Basic Records from the 1970 Census: Description and Technical Documentation. Washington, D.C.: Government Printing Office.

U.S. , Bureau of the Census, and Bureau of Labor Statistics. 1976. "Concepts and Methods Used in Labor Statistics Derived from the Current Population Survey. " Current Population Reports, Series P-23, no. 62. Washington, D.C.: Government Printing Office.

U.S., Department of Health, Education and Welfare. 1973. Work in America. Report of a Special Task Force to the Secretary of Health, Education and Welfare. Cambridge, Mass.: MIT Press.

U.S., Department of Labor, Employment and Training Administration. 1979. Employment and Training Report of the President. Washington, D.C.: Government Printing Office.

_____. 1976. Employment and Training Report of the President. Washington, D.C.: Government Printing Office.

U.S., Department of Labor, Manpower Administration. 1974. "Youth and the Meaning of Work." Manpower Research Monograph No. 32. Washington, D.C.: Government Printing Office.

_____. 1972. Handbook for Analyzing Jobs. Washington, D.C.: Government Printing Office.

_____. 1971. Relating General Educational Development to Career Planning. Washington, D.C.: Government Printing Office.

U.S., Employment Service. 1977. Dictionary of Occupational Titles. 4th ed. Washington, D.C.: Government Printing Office.

_____. 1966. Selected Characteristics of Occupations (Physical Demands, Working Conditions, Training Time). Supplement to the Dictionary of Occupational Titles, 3d ed. Washington, D.C.: Government Printing Office.

_____. 1965. Dictionary of Occupational Titles. 2 vols. 3d ed. Washington, D.C.: Government Printing Office.

U.S. News and World Report. 1972. November 27, pp. 48-49.

Vitiemo, Tullio. 1980. "How Valuable Is a College Degree?" Columbus Dispatch, June 2, p. B-2.

Vroom, Victor H. 1964. Work and Motivation. New York: John Wiley & Sons.

Wachter, Michael L. 1974. "Primary and Secondary Labor Markets: A Critique of the Dual Approach." Brookings Papers on Economic Activity, no. 3, pp. 637-80.

Walker, Charles R. , and Robert H. Guest. 1952. The Man on the Assembly Line. Cambridge, Mass.: Harvard University Press.

Walton, Richard E. 1974. "Alienation and Innovation in the Workplace." In Work and the Quality of Life, edited by James O'Toole, pp. 227-45. Cambridge, Mass.: MIT University Press.

Welch, Finis. 1979. "Effects of Cohort Size on Earnings: The Baby Boom Babies' Financial Bust." Journal of Political Economy 87: S65-97.

_____. 1970. "Education in Production." Journal of Political Economy 78 (January-February): 35-59.

Welch, Finis, and William Gould. 1976. "An Experience Imputation or an Imputation Experience." Mimeographed. Santa Monica, Calif.: Rand Corporation.

Withey, Stephen B. , et al. 1971. A Degree and What Else? New York: McGraw-Hill.

Yankelovich, Daniel. 1974. The New Morality: A Profile of American Youth in the 70's. New York: McGraw-Hill.

Zonana, Victor F. 1975. "Battle of the Bulge: Firms Fight Effect of 1950s Baby Boom." Wall Street Journal, August 18, pp. 1, 21.

INDEX

absenteeism, 104, 112-14, 122
Andrisani, P. J., 104
Aronowitz, S., 69, 118, 123

Baran, P. A., 36
Beck, E. M., 31
Becker, G. S., 3, 6, 16, 21, 23, 24
Bedrosian, H., 108
Behn, W. H., 123, 124, 128
benefits, 6, 7, 23, 26, 118; private, 3, 5, 117, 126; social, 3, 5
Ben-Porath, Y., 23
Berg, I., 17, 66, 71, 78, 97, 106, 108, 127
Bielby, W. T., 13
Bienstock, P., 120, 121
Bird, C., 4
Bisconti, A. S., 17, 107
Blau, P. M., 3
Blaug, M., 6
Blauner, R., 116
Borglum, R. P., 116
Bowen, H. R., 6, 126
Bowles, S., 29, 34-35, 36, 40, 126, 128
Bowman, M. J., 6
Braverman, H., 33, 40, 67, 119, 123, 128
Brown, C. A., 113

Cain, G. C., 30, 32
capitalism, 31, 33-34, 36-37, 39, 67, 116, 119, 123-24, 125
Carnegie Commission on Higher Education, 3, 127
Carnoy, M., 31, 32, 121
Carter, M., 31
census, 53-56, 60-61, 62, 69, 98

Chadwick-Jones, J. K., 113
changes in the workplace: cooperatives, 121-22, 123; industrial democracy, 121; job enlargement, 120, 122; job enrichment, 120; job redesign, 120, 122-23; job rotation, 120, 123; participatory management, 121; political, 120, 121, 122, 124; technical, 120, 122-23, 124
Chiswick, B. R., 23
Coburn, D., 111
Cohn, E., 6, 22
college graduates, 3-4, 6-7, 9, 15, 17, 22, 24, 26, 28-29, 32, 38, 58, 62-63, 68, 72, 97, 102, 107-8, 118, 126-27
cooperatives, 121-22, 123
costs, 6-7, 23, 24, 25, 26-27, 38, 118; direct, 6, 22; indirect, 6, 22; private, 126; social, 7
credential effect, 17, 26-27, 90
crime, 6, 7
Current Population Survey (CPS), 52, 53, 54-56, 60-62

D'Amico, R. J., 31
Davis, L. E., 120
Denison, E. F., 6
Diamond, D. E., 108
Dictionary of Occupational Titles (DOT), 17, 47-48, 52, 53-56, 60-62, 70-72, 91
discrimination, 28, 30
Doeringer, P. B., 30
drug problems, 104, 113
Duncan, G. J., 9
Duncan, O. D., 3
Dunham, R. B., 120

political participation, 6, 7
Porter, L. W. , 109-10, 113
private sector, 119-24
productivity, 9, 23, 25, 26, 37,
 38, 46, 104, 118, 120, 121, 124
public policy, 124-27

Quinn, R. P. , 17, 104, 105, 107,
 113

rate-of-return, 6-7, 8, 9-10; pri-
 vate, 6, 10, 26, 28, 118; social,
 7, 10, 26, 28, 118
Rawlins, V. L. , 17, 127
Reich, M. , 30-31
Rosen, S. , 23
Rosenberg, R. D. , 121
Rosenstein, E. , 121
Rumberger, R. W. , 10, 31-32

salary (see pecuniary returns)
Schultz, T. W. , 21, 22
Scoville, J. G. , 53, 64, 80
Sexton, P. C. , 66
Shearer, D. , 121
Shepard, J. M. , 68-69, 116
Shepard, L. J. , 113
Sheppard, H. L. , 107-8
skill requirements, 15, 16-17,
 26, 38, 45-47, 59-60, 61, 63,
 66; changes in, 52, 57, 59, 61-
 62, 67-72, 91, 96-98; distribution of, 57, 68, 69, 75, 76-78,
 84, 86, 91
skills: discrepancy with education, 4-5, 6-7, 15-18, 23, 39,
 45, 58, 68, 74-96, 97-98, 102,
 104, 105, 107, 112, 113-14,
 116, 117, 118, 121-22; distribution of, 69, 71-72; general types
 of, 15, 16, 22-23, 46, 48, 64,
 67, 97; specific types of, 22-24,
 46, 48-49, 52, 64, 127; utilization of, 5, 6-7, 8, 15-17, 23,
 32, 34, 38, 45, 119

Slocum, J. W. , 110
Smith, J. P. , 10, 24
Snyderman, B. , 105
Solmon, L. C. , 17, 107
Sorensen, A. B. , 104, 105
specific vocational preparation
 (SVP), 48, 49, 54, 55, 63, 64
Spence, M. , 25-26
Spenner, K. I. , 62
Srivastva, S. , 107, 110
Staines, G. L. , 17
State of California, Employment
 Development Department, 66
Steers, R. M. , 113
Strauss, G. , 19, 107
strike activity, 7, 104, 116
Sturmthal, A. F. , 123
substitution, 20, 21, 22, 27
Sutermeister, R. A. , 106, 109,
 110

Taubman, P. , 9, 26
Taylor, J. C. , 120
technical changes, 120, 122-23,
 124
technology, 28, 29, 31, 32, 34,
 38-39, 57, 67, 69
Temme, L. V. , 52-53
Thompson, D. E. , 116
Thurow, L. C. , 27-29
Time, 125
Tolbert, C. M. , 31
Trent, J. W. , 10
turnover, 104, 113-14, 121, 124

Ulman, L. , 17, 127
unions, 119, 122, 123
U.S. , Bureau of the Census, 19,
 47, 51-52, 61
U.S. , Bureau of the Census and
 Bureau of Labor Statistics, 61
U.S. , Bureau of Labor Statistics,
 6-7, 15, 17, 18, 52, 66, 91, 125
U.S. , Department of Health, Edu-
 cation and Welfare, 33, 101, 121

ABOUT THE AUTHOR

RUSSELL W. RUMBERGER is Research Associate at the Institute for Research on Educational Finance and Governance, Stanford University. He is also affiliated with the Center for Economic Studies, Palo Alto, California. Formerly, he was a Senior Research Associate at the Center for Human Resource Research, Ohio State University, Columbus, Ohio. He has served as a consultant to UNESCO, the State of California, the Inter-American Development Bank, and the National Institute of Education.

He has published articles in professional journals of economics and education, including the Journal of Human Resources and the Cambridge Journal of Economics.

He received a B.S. in Electrical Engineering from Carnegie-Mellon University in 1971, an M.A. in Economics from Stanford University in 1978, and a Ph.D. in Education from Stanford University in 1978.